# The Forest for the Trees

TB119147

# The Forest
# for the Trees

## How Humans
## Shaped the
## North Woods

JEFF FORESTER

MINNESOTA HISTORICAL SOCIETY PRESS

© 2004 by the Minnesota Historical Society. All rights reserved. No part of this book may be used or reproduced in any manner whatsoever without written permission except in the case of brief quotations embodied in critical articles and reviews. For information, write to the Minnesota Historical Society Press, 345 Kellogg Blvd. W., St. Paul, MN 55102-1906.

www.mhspress.org

The Minnesota Historical Society Press is a member of the
Association of American University Presses.

Manufactured in the United States of America

10 9 8 7 6 5 4 3 2 1

∞ The paper used in this publication meets the minimum requirements of the American National Standard for Information Sciences—Permanence for Printed Library Materials, ANSI Z39.48-1984.

International Standard Book Number
ISBN-10: 0-87351-650-8 (paper)
ISBN-13: 978-0-87351-650-1 (paper)

Library of Congress Cataloging-in-Publication Data

Forester, Jeff (Jeffery Edward), 1961–
    The forest for the trees : how humans shaped the North woods / Jeff Forester.
    p. cm.
Includes bibliographical references (p. ).
ISBN 0-87351-480-7 (casebound : alk. paper)
    1. Forests and forestry—Minnesota—Boundary Waters Canoe Area—History.
    2. Forest ecology—Minnesota—Boundary Waters Canoe Area—History.
    3. Nature—Effect of human beings on—Minnesota—Boundary Waters Canoe Area—
       History.
    4. Boundary Waters Canoe Area (Minn.)—History.
    I. Title.

SD144.M6F67 2004
634.9'09776'75—dc22

                                                                                    2004000164

Frontispiece: Railroad tracks cut through misty pines at Herb Good's Fourmile Portage

*For Allie,*
*who dances up the steepest paths*
*and shines in the darkest nights*

## THE TIGER

TIGER, tiger, burning bright
In the forests of the night,
What immortal hand or eye
Could frame thy fearful symmetry?

In what distant deeps or skies
Burnt the fire of thine eyes?
On what wings dare he aspire?
What the hand dare seize the fire?

And what shoulder and what art
Could twist the sinews of thy heart?
And, when thy heart began to beat,
What dread hand and what dread feet?

What the hammer? What the chain?
In what furnace was thy brain?
What the anvil? What dread grasp
Dare its deadly terrors clasp?

When the stars threw down their spears,
And water'd heaven with their tears,
Did He smile His work to see?
Did He who made the lamb make thee?

Tiger, tiger, burning bright
In the forests of the night,
What immortal hand or eye
Dare frame thy fearful symmetry?

WILLIAM BLAKE

# The Forest for the Trees

# Preface and Acknowledgments

IN SEPTEMBER 1991 I began the research for an ecological history of northern Minnesota, but my association with the region began at birth. My great-grandfather was one of the first emigrants to northern Minnesota, a Cornish mining engineer who hiked over the Vermilion Trail to begin the digs at Tower. I remember going for long walks with my grandmother, Theresa (Treat) Jeffery, and being rapt as she bent slowly to pick a wintergreen leaf (tastes like Beemans gum, she'd say), or blueberries, or some fantastic mushroom, or a ginseng root shaped like a little man, or a wildflower. To her the forest was a large garden, ordered, full of useful plants and beautiful flowers. I followed behind, listening as she talked about the forest and about the history of the land.

My grandmother was very active in the St. Louis County Historical Society and the Tower Historical Society. The Railroad Train Museum at the entrance to Tower is dedicated to her memory. She was instrumental in setting up the underground mine at Soudan, and trips into the mine my great-grandfather had opened remain a favored rainy-day activity. This book is largely the result of the wonderful walks she and I took together, and the stories that she told of forest fires, of voyageurs, Indians, miners, and loggers.

The Winton watershed—the streams and lakes that flow from the northern slopes of the Laurentian Divide, up the Stony River, into Fall Lake and north through the border lakes, and into Quetico Provincial Park in Canada—defined my study area. Because pioneer loggers used water routes to transport logs to the mill, examining a single watershed is especially instructive.

I concentrated the research for this book in five source areas, conducted close to forty interviews with those who still had a memory of the logging days, and read oral histories of fifty more who had died before I began this work. I reviewed the archives of the main players, the lumber companies, the U.S. Forest Service, and county, state, and federal documents. I used the local newspapers from that time. The works of researchers who had gone before me, the perspectives of many historians, and academic works that touched upon my topic were also a great help.

The rotting dams, sluiceways, and trestle pilings, the scarcity of old white pine, the diseased "flag" limbs of the trees that survived, the tangled thickets of vigorous, young aspen stands, the absence of elk and caribou, the abundance of deer, the portages and roads, the diminished town of Winton—all of these informed me.

I am indebted to all who took the time to talk with me. One of the greatest joys of this work was meeting and speaking at great length with these people, many of whom are now deceased: the late Robert G. Whiteside and his wife, Kitty, E. Matt Laitala, the late Dorothy Anderson, Robert and Opal Hill, Mrs. Howard Hario, Cyrille Fortier Jr., James Pete, the late Mary Anderson, the late Andy and Hannah Johnson, Robert Mills, the late Miron "Bud" Heinselman, the late J. C. "Buzz" Ryan, Cecilia Kuitenen, the late Harry Homer, John Sansted, Lou Gold, Tuano Maki, Rudolph and Auggie Majerla, Robert Porthan, Everett Laitala, and Urho Hokkanen. I also thank the late Lee Brownell for his many excellent photographs; Mr. and Mrs. Ralph Tuthill for not only their photographs but also their excellent coffee; and Victor Zyganor (Whitewater Slim) for his spirit, his egg coffee, and his authentic lumberjack lemon cream pie, baked in an old lumber camp wood stove. A very special thanks to the late Laurie McGuinn for not only her invaluable help with the labor section but also her support and warm friendship. Thanks also to Nancy Lincoln, a partner in this effort, who transcribed many of these interviews.

The patience, helpfulness, and professionalism of the Minnesota Historical Society's staff cannot be overstated. I am deeply indebted to editor Shannon M. Pennefeather, whose help during the revision process was indispensable and whose many creative suggestions made this a much better book. Her enthusiasm and kind, challenging, and detailed editing carried this project through to a far happier end.

The staff of the Iron Range Interpretive Center was very helpful and knowledgeable; Edward Nelson oversees an excellent organization there. The Lake County Historical Society, the Iron Range Historical Society, the Ely/Winton Historical Society, the St. Louis County Historical Society, and the Vermilion Interpretive Center and their staffs provided substantial assistance for my research. I thank the U.S. Forest Service for considerable time and assistance, especially Mary Shedd, Ralphe Bonde, and Walter Okstad. Mr. Okstad offered an invaluable starting point for me and was of untold assistance in providing information, guidance, and support. Tim Loesch at the Minnesota Department of Natural Resources provided much assistance with the vegetation type maps contained in this book.

The *Tower News* in Tower, Minnesota, supplied material from the *Vermilion Iron Journal*. Tony Sikora, his wife, Lisa, and news editor Phyllis Burgess made me a guest in their busy office for weeks on end. Mr. Sikora, an area historian in his own right, graciously agreed to review this manuscript in its various forms and offered excellent suggestions for its improvement.

A special thanks is due another area historian: scientist and writer Milton Stenlund, whose books were of infinite assistance and editorial comments of great value. Howard Libes, Dr. David Zaber, and Jim Berg, old writing allies of mine, read and reread early drafts of this work. Their assistance was critical as I tried to separate the wheat from the chaff.

I am deeply grateful to Dale (Bo) and Bunny Wiersema, our neighbors on Fall Lake, at the very edge of the Boundary Waters Canoe Area Wilderness, where my wife and I lived during much of this project. Northern Minnesota can seem a cold and inhospitable place, especially in the winter and particularly to folks newly arrived from warmer climes. Bo and Bunny warmed our hearts and fed our spirits on many a long, dark night. Gratitude also to Lee Roy (Pee Wee) Maki and Shirley Kidd for opening their hearts and homes to us. The chance to get to know them was one of the happiest aspects of this work.

# The Forest for the Trees

# Introduction

*We do not see things as they are*
*we see them as we are*

TALMUDIC SAYING

COLONIAL AMERICANS stood on the eastern rim of a remarkable plat-
ter, a cornucopia heaped with riches: minerals ranging from gold to the
world's most valuable iron, wild game for both food and fur, the as-
tounding Atlantic and Great Lakes fisheries, plains with rich topsoil
three feet deep, waterways for shipping and power, coal and oil for fuel,
and wood to make all manner of implement—road, boat, bridge,
wagon, cart—wood for building, for cooking, for heating, for industrial
fuel. This wealth of wood was available in such abundance as to be almost free, at a time when technology allowed consumption at rates
never before known. Wood provided the base for American infrastructure, and upon this foundation Americans built the most successful
economy in the world.[1]

Logging technology was unchanged from Roman times, yet Americans consumed twenty-five thousand square miles of forest in their first
one hundred years, burning most of it to make clearings and then planting crops around the charred stumps. Anthropomorphic fire defined
the advancing line of settlement. Puritanical roots tempered colonial
vision, and early Americans cleared the forests with religious and moral
purpose. In the well-ordered, pastoral conversion of the forest to culti-

3

vated land, early Americans saw virtue. There was no cry for conservation then, no ethic promoting the preservation of wildland, the suppression of fire, or the conservation of resources.[2]

Of all the standing timber in the United States before white settlement, four-fifths of it grew on the eastern third of the country. Every day for fifty years Americans cut more than one hundred square miles of forest for fuel. The average cabin burned more than its weight in wood—from twenty to forty cords—each year. Most colonies had at least a few one-thousand-ton ironworks, each of which consumed between twenty and thirty thousand acres of forest annually. Every year the rate of deforestation accelerated.[3]

Americans burned most of the timber east of the Mississippi River. While lightning-caused fire was always a threat, in the East it usually came during thunderstorms, accompanied by rain. Additionally, thunderstorms were common at times of high humidity and did not usually occur in the early spring or late fall, when the forests were driest. Cook fires, campfires, sparks from railroad engines, and field clearing accounted for most of the huge wildfires that swept back and forth along the line of civilization.

By the 1850s, timber was scarce in the East. By 1869, two hundred and fifty years after the harvest began, the U.S. Department of Agriculture reported that the Northeast harvested 2.4 billion board feet of white pine while the estimate for the Lake States was 2.7 billion board feet. Michigan sawed 1.7 billion board feet of white pine lumber that year alone. In 1889, Michigan, Wisconsin, and Minnesota cut 9.9 billion board feet, 36.9 percent of the nation's production. In a U.S. Department of Agriculture report, R. V. Reynolds wrote: "Lumber is the choicest part of the forest crop, because it comes principally from large dimension and high-grade material. 75% of the lumber cut, and fully 90% of high-quality lumber is taken from old trees. The search for virgin timber explains why the lumber industry has migrated from one region to another."[4]

On April 4, 1889, the *Vermilion Iron Journal*, the new weekly paper of Tower, Minnesota, situated at the edge of the immense and unexplored border lakes region, reprinted a portentous piece from the *Chicago Tim-*

*berman:* "It is said that within a few hundred miles of Duluth the greatest pine forest now extant east of the Pacific Coast are to be found." The lake country of northern Minnesota was in fact the largest remaining uncut cache of eastern white pine in the world. The pine was a relatively new arrival in the area, moving west due to changes in weather patterns and tribal fire regimes. White pine is fire dependent, and tribal anthropomorphic fire played a role in its propagation, distribution, and size. The clearing of this forest would be the final pioneer harvest in the lower forty-eight states, beginning just before the tools and efficiencies of the industrial revolution made their way into the woods.

The last pioneer logger in the lower forty-eight states was probably Robert Whiteside, and as pioneers went, he was a dandy: intelligent, rugged, independent, visionary, and exceptionally lucky. Whiteside and his brothers John, Job, and Richard and brothers-in-law John Densmore and Edward Robinson began the cut on the Winton watershed in northern Minnesota, but they would not finish the chore. Just as the Whitesides arrived on the scene, technological improvements greatly enhanced the logger's ability to alter the landscape. As the transportation routes, communication channels, and new industrialized corporate structures became better developed, logging operations changed, and family outfits like Whiteside's had a difficult time competing. Lumber baron Frederick Weyerhaeuser would finish the cut in the border lakes.

During the nineteenth century, railroads, telegraph lines, canals, river locks, and improved waterway channels made possible the United States' highly integrated market economy and commodity markets. When Frederick Weyerhaeuser added the raw power of industrialization to the mix in the mid-nineteenth century, the pace of the cut in Michigan, Wisconsin, and most of Minnesota was akin to a North Dakota combine sweeping through winter wheat. The already remarkable and unprecedented American tree harvest multiplied six-fold.[5]

The industrialization of logging operations in the border lakes happened more slowly than in other places, however, because of the region's rugged ridges, tangles of thorn and brush, fierce winds, and numbing cold. Its natural transportation routes, the rivers, flow north, away from civilization. Thousands of lakes break up the landscape and make road building very difficult. Thus, the Arrowhead's natural defenses held while more accessible forests fell. It was at this time, before the Arrowhead was cut but after the East's forests were gone and the Upper Midwest mostly cleared, that many Americans began to develop a new land ethic, a shift away from the Puritanical view that favored the wanton clearing of forests.

Of six land-management paradigms, each is evident in northern Minnesota: the *tribal,* where the Ojibwe—and the Dakota before them, and others before them—flamed the forests to increase blueberry yields or to cultivate wild rice paddies, to control insects, to create grassy meadows as forage for elk, caribou, and moose, or as a weapon in warfare; the *pioneer* stage, marked by small, independent operators, families like Robert Whiteside and his brothers; the *industrial* stage, during which the harvest rate accelerated and lumber barons like Weyerhaeuser used railroads, steam crawlers, and other mechanization to fell trees, mill lumber, and ship it to market; the *conservation* phase, during which far-thinking men like Bernard Fernow and Gifford Pinchot recognized the strategic importance of forests and tried to manage them the way a farmer manages a bean field, save with a rotation of one hundred years instead of one hundred days.

Beginning in the 1920s, however, men like Christopher C. Andrews, Ernest Oberholtzer, Sigurd Olson, and Aldo Leopold came to see values in the forest even greater than timber production: recreation and spiritual renewal. Since its creation in 1909, recreation has always generated more money than timber receipts in Superior National Forest. So began the *wilderness ethic,* the idea that some land should be held in its primeval state. Like Fernow and Pinchot, these men struggled for a long time before there was any practical expression of their ideas on the ground. In the 1960s, U.S. Forest Service (USFS) researcher Miron "Bud" Heinselman recognized the scientific values of a "virgin" landscape as a baseline. His ideas fueled a grassroots wilderness effort, and in 1978 logging ended on much of the Winton watershed, what had become the Boundary Waters Canoe Area Wilderness (BWCAW).

Heinselman went further than the early wilderness advocates, promoting what has come to be known as *restoration forestry*. It was not enough to set aside wilderness; Heinselman and others urged that steps be taken to undo the negative impacts of the pioneers, the industrialists, the conservationists. One of the biggest negative impacts, Heinselman noted wryly, was that fire had been excluded from the BWCAW for half a century. His research proved that fire had always been a part of the border lakes' ecosystem, and since its artificial suppression—a tenet of the conservationists—the forest had grown up into a highly flammable thicket. By the 1970s fuel loads were close to twenty times higher than in pre-settlement times. Heinselman recommended that the USFS set prescribed burns in the BWCAW to decrease these fuel loads.

Forest service policymakers, however, interpreted the Wilderness Act—passed by Congress in 1964 to define and preserve the nation's wilderness—to mean that the land had been truly set aside and all activity save camping was excluded. They banned not only logging, road building, and mechanized travel, but also tree planting, mechanical thinning, and prescribed burns. Campers could use only downed wood for campfires and could not cut any standing dead trees.

Despite growing scientific evidence that fire suppression was damaging the system, USFS policymakers remained inflexible in their reading of the Wilderness Act. They relented only recently, when fuel loads in the BWCAW became so dangerously high that a cataclysm of biblical proportions threatened. On July 4, 1999, a windstorm leveled about five hundred thousand acres of trees along the U.S.–Canada border. Fuel levels jumped to 120 times historic levels. A fire fed by a fuel load of this magnitude would be so large and terrible—with burning gasses reaching twenty to thirty thousand feet high and indrafts of up to ninety miles an hour—that no organization could hope to control it. Fire experts predicted a veritable tornado of flame, a firestorm that would create its own weather pattern and could easily overrun local communities.

Policymakers were forced, with nature doing the arm-twisting, to do what Heinselman had urged forty years before. On September 16, 2002, the USFS set fire to the wilderness, the first efforts at restorative forestry by a federal agency on a designated wilderness area in the United States, although the goal was public safety, not ecological preservation. The door is open, though, and many hope that once the immediate threat is mitigated the controlled burning will continue.

Each of these six land-management paradigms shows on the landscape in northern Minnesota. Each was a reaction to a specific social need during a particular time. Early conservation efforts, the wilderness movement, and restoration forestry were all attempts to respond to a dwindling resource base, whether the resource was trees, recreation, genetic material, or, perhaps most importantly, a valid baseline for scientific inquiry.

This book chronicles the transitions from tribal land managers to pioneer loggers like Robert Whiteside, to lumber barons like Frederick Weyerhaeuser, to conservationists Pinchot and Fernow, to wilderness advocates Oberholtzer and Leopold, and finally to the restoration land management ideas of Bud Heinselman. The frame that the United States placed around mere rock, water, and tree has changed dramatically since 1891, when Whiteside arrived in the area, until today when forest service crews set restorative fires in the wilderness. The land itself, indifferent, immutable, and eternal, has remained. Only in the artificial structure of laws—each reflecting the social needs of the time in which it was written—is the land different.

Ely's ecological history, the tribal, pioneer, boom, and conservation phases, the radical mutation to designated wilderness, and finally the intentional burning of that wilderness, are like menhirs: each a kiosk left to mark Americans' evolving relationship with the land. Once a mining and lumbering town, Ely is now the canoe capital of the world, home to polar explorers Paul Schurke and Will Steger, wilderness writers like Jim Dale Vickery, photographers like Jim Brandenburg, outfitters and sportsmen. George Stuntz, surveyor of much of northern Minnesota, predicted that the forests and minerals there would make the Arrowhead "the economic heart of the continent." Today the Ely Chamber of Commerce has a new slogan: "Gateway to the Wilderness." There is a brisk local industry in the manufacture and sale of outdoor clothing and camping gadgetry, as well as guided "eco-adventure" trips to destinations beyond the BWCAW, in other wilderness areas in Belize, Argentina, Chile, New Zealand, and Africa. Ely is home to the International Wolf Center, where L. David Mech, the world's pre-eminent wolf biologist, bases his Eastern timber wolf (*Canis lupus lycaon*) research. Lynn Rogers made Ely the focus for his important studies of the black bear (*Ursus americanus*). Now, it is the act of not logging, of not mining, of not trapping, of not developing the land that butters Ely's bread.

Northern Minnesota is not the only place where restoration, tree planting, brush thinning, and controlled prescribed fire is necessary to bring the landscape back into what biologists call the Historic Range of Natural Variability. It is simply the first place where fuel loads became so critically high and the biota so far out of balance that restoration via prescribed burning was the only management option. There are many eyes watching the fires burn in northern Minnesota. Once again, human activities there represent a watermark in our evolving relationship with the land.

# 1

## Rock, Water, Tree

*I want to tell what the forests*
*were like*
*I will have to speak*
*in a forgotten language*

      W. S. MERWIN, "Witness"

---

THIS IS THE STORY of the changing of a landscape, the Arrowhead of Minnesota, and how that landscape changed us. It is difficult to study the ecological history of the BWCAW without looking at the human history there, for the two are symbiotic. Karl Marx recognized this in *Grundrisse*, writing, "As societies try to remake nature, they remake themselves, without ever really escaping natural influences." The fortunes of one, the land, are conjoined with the fortunes of the other, the people. The border region is rock, water, and tree. Two dynamic forces, fire and ice, dominate its history and define human interaction with this place.

The bedrock is ancient. Some of the oldest exposed surface outcroppings on the planet, more than 3.5 billion years old, bulge through the earth's crust here. While the rock is ancient, the land and wildlife are almost infantile. The last glacier retreated from the Arrowhead just twelve thousand years ago, and its passing is still fresh on the land. The ice drove southwest from Hudson Bay in slabs two miles thick, gouging and crushing the land like a bulldozer. It scoured northern Minnesota, plowing up soil and soft rocks, roiling the turbid debris south to Iowa, Illinois, and Wisconsin, and depositing the rubble in steep terminal moraines. The bony spine of North America lay vivisected in its wake.

The ice retreated to the Arctic, but the melt remained, creating the border lakes, thirty thousand of them, resting in clean bedrock basins. The action of the ice shows clearly on aerial photographs: the border lakes lie vaguely northeast and spread southwest from Hudson Bay across the Canadian border and into northern Minnesota. Lake Superior is the largest of these, its rugged north shore the remnant of ancient mountains. The Laurentian Divide extends over the north side of the Great Lakes, follows Superior's north shore down to Duluth, and then strikes off vaguely northwest to the Canadian Rockies. North of this continental divide the surface waters flow up the maze of lakes and rivers in the border country, through Canadian boreal forests, and across tundra where even the stalwart black spruce cannot grow, to Hudson Bay and the Arctic Ocean. To the south the waters flow either to the Great Lakes or down the Mississippi and so to the Atlantic.

The Ojibwe call the divide *In-ni-wis-ti-go-ma*, translating to "here the waters run two ways," and they named the Arrowhead region *Mesaba*, meaning "grandmother of them all" or "sleeping giant." North of the Laurentian, the mean yearly temperature is just thirty-six degrees Fahrenheit. Frost often comes in August, and snow usually covers the ground from November through late April, with yearly accumulations averaging sixty inches. Violent thunderstorms are common the rest of the year. The lowest recorded temperature was minus sixty degrees on February 2, 1996, while the record high occurred on July 6, 1936, when temperatures blazed to 114, a fluctuation of 174 degrees.

The weight of the ice compressed the Canadian Shield hundreds of feet. Since then, as the elastic rock expands, Superior, Wisconsin, rises as much as one-half inch each year. Glaciers scattered house-sized erratics across the northland. Rocks embedded in the ice cut parallel striations in the bedrock as they passed, creating scars that in some places still appear fresh. Sand or clay mixed in the ice polished other rocks smooth. Glaciers left the border lakes region without compromise: it is either water or rock. The forests are almost accidental, clinging to narrow belts of rubble, sand, clay, or loam where meager soils have accumulated in shallow basins. The last virgin tracts of eastern white pine in the world grew stubbornly on this marginalized scree.[1]

Remnant white pine communities survived the last ice age on transient islands in the Atlantic, rock piles exposed as sea levels fell while ice accumulated on land. When the ice melted and the water rose, white pine spread to the mainland and took hold. Postglacial fossil records show white pine in the Shenandoah Valley of Virginia 12,700 years ago. From there the tree spread northward. The species colonized Virginia and western Maryland and then moved north and west along the high, cool Appalachians, reaching northern New England ten thou-

*In the Winton watershed, second-growth forest clings to rocky, glaciated soil.*

sand years ago. In the next thousand years white pine spread on the north and south shores of the St. Lawrence River, the Thousand Island chain, Lake Ontario, Lake Erie, Lake Huron, Lake Michigan, and Lake Superior, arriving in Minnesota seven thousand years ago. For a time white pine grew much farther north than it does today, but the "little ice age" of 1550 to 1880 decreased its northern range. It was still spreading slowly westward in the 1880s, when Robert Whiteside and his brothers arrived and began the cut.[2]

*Pinus strobus*, eastern white pine, towers above other trees in the forest, rising to more than 225 feet. These trees can live half a millennium, reaching diameters of more than six feet, their trunks enormous, living cathedral pilasters, their crowns the spires. The needles grow in follicles of five up to five inches long, their pale, silvery-green color giving a moonlit appearance even in daylight. The tree's grain is clean, the wood soft and easily worked. Yet it is tenacious: white pine lumber resists creeping moistures, the bite of winter, the warping heat of summer. And pine logs are more buoyant than other species, easily floating down waterways to sawmills. For these reasons white pine was the most valuable species to pioneer loggers. Happily for them, white pine once dominated the forests from Newfoundland and eastern Manitoba southward to the Appalachians and west to Iowa.[3]

Unlike in New England, the forest in northern Minnesota was not an unbroken sea of pine. The topography of rock, water, and glacial soils and the effects of fire worked to create a mosaic of forest on the Arrowhead. It is a complex area ecologically, an ecotone, a transition zone between the hardwood and white pine forests of the Great Lakes and the boreal forests, aspen and spruce, of the subarctic. The dark and solemn cathedral-like lines of near-black pine trunks slowly gave way in places to mixed stands of strikingly white paper birch (*Betula Alleghaniensis*), blue-green spruce (*Picea glavca*), and silver and sweet-smelling white cedar (*Thuja occidentalis*). In the late fall, October or early November, the tamaracks flamed imperial gold and shed their needles. Nevertheless, large, old white pine trees dominated the Winton watershed at the time Robert Whiteside arrived.

In 1895, after years of logging, cruisers estimated that the land north of Duluth still contained more than 40 billion board feet of standing pine. Between 1880 and 1920, loggers cut about 2.5 billion board feet of white pine off the Winton watershed. The few small pockets of original white pine forest in the BWCAW that survived until wilderness designation protected them from logging are no larger than ten acres. Most of the trees are younger than two hundred and fifty years, though the oldest stand, a group of red and white pine on Three Mile Island in Sea Gull Lake, began growing around 1595. Many of these blew down in the July 4, 1999, storm, and in 2002 the USFS burned the island. Still, some fifteen-hundred-year-old cedar trees and a handful of the old red and white pine survived.[4]

Lumbermen spared the few remnant pine stands for a variety of practical reasons. Some were small, isolated stands surrounded by acres of lower-value trees. Some grew on windy ridges which cautious fellers saved for still days that never came. Some grew at the bottom of steep gullies. Sometimes a company could not finish clearing an area before the weather turned warm and broke up the ice roads, and, if the stands were small in acreage, the company never returned for them. The loggers also left the diseased and the fire-damaged, but most of the remnant old growth trees that live today were simply too small to bother with a hundred years ago.

There is one such stand off the Echo Trail, not far from Ely, along the shores of Hegeman Lake. The USFS estimates that the trees began growing after a fire in 1835 and were a mere sixty years old when Robert Whiteside began his operations. The pines are not great in girth, more like skinny teenagers, but they are much taller than other northland trees. The lower branches have withered from lack of sun, leaving the trunks straight and clean. Far above, 150 to 200 feet, the crowns wave gently in the wind, a silvery-green canopy. Underneath, at relatively even spacing, an understory of birch, balsam fir, spruce, red maple, basswood, and red oak grows in the dappled light. The forest floor is clear and open, almost manicured, like a park. In the summer the temperature is cooler under the old pine trees, and in the winter, when the wind roars far overhead in the crowns, it is still and warmer below. Black trunks, straight, clean pillars, rise along each side of the trail. The stand is quiet, inspiring the awe intrinsic to great age or beauty and compelling one to speak in whispers, as if in a church.

These cathedral groves are rare in northern Minnesota. Short-lived transitional species—balsam poplar (*Populus balsamifera*), bigtooth aspen (*Populus grandidentata*), and quaking aspen (*Populus tremoloides*)—dominate the forest that grew up after loggers cut out the pine. After ninety years of USFS fire suppression programs, woody debris litters the forest floor. Even in old-growth groves like Hegeman Lake, the flammable balsam fir and spruce understory can quickly carry fire into the treetops, destroying the stand.

Many people think of a forest fire as a wild conflagration destroying everything in its path, what is known as catastrophic fire. This is the fire that makes the evening news, the fire that we read about in the paper, the fire that most urbanites, now living in a fireless world, know. Catastrophic fires spread through the tops, or crowns, of trees, the canopy, and are common to younger, more flammable stands of jack or red pine or transitional aspen, where the crowns and lower branches are closer to the ground and ignite more easily. When a fire moved from the ground to the crown, the loggers called, "She's covering," and got out of the way, for once a fire reaches the treetops, wind drives it and it moves more quickly. These are also known as stand-replacing fires because instead of culling undergrowth and dead and downed timber, canopy fires typically kill all forest cover. Usually a species other than the original stand dominates after such a fire. But in the border lakes, catastrophic fires were not historically predominant.[5]

Fire was always an integral and natural part of the white pine forest, determining the species, age, and successional stages of the forest as well as the wildlife. Virtually all of the BWCAW has burned from one to three times in the last four hundred years. The white pine forests cleared by logging might well have been even older, but the record was lost when the trees were removed. The catastrophic fires that followed logging operations in the early days and threaten the area today are not natural. Most natural fires in old-growth forests, especially white pine stands, do not cover.[6]

The relative humidity is higher in older stands, the wind less intense, the fuel sparse. Thus fires typically smolder along the ground, clearing out downed wood, shrub, spruce, balsam, and poplar seedlings—the boreal forest component and fuels that dominate today. These low, creeping fires occurred, on an average acre, about once every thirty-six years, removing fuel that could cause canopy-killing fires, thereby perpetuating older stands. The old white pine, their corky bark sixteen inches thick and branches over one hundred feet off the ground, survived most of these fires undamaged save for trunk scars. White pine seedlings do well in the shady, cleared areas under their parents once fire removes the boreal competition. Further, fire prepares a site for the seeds to germinate, as they will only take root and survive if they grow directly on the soil, not in a leafy duff.[7]

Periodically, when weather conditions were perfect—relative humidity below 30 percent and winds exceeding fifteen to twenty miles per hour—some natural fires did cover, destroying portions of white pine stands. These natural crown fires tended to visit the stands once every three hundred years, with older stands surviving in areas that were more protected from fire by wetlands, lakes, or other natural barriers. Because the prevailing winds in northern Minnesota are from west to east, large bodies of north-to-south-oriented waters tended to shield stands from large fires. Jackfish and Pipestone Bays on Basswood Lake, along with the Horse Lake chain, Birch Lake, and the Stony River are all such natural barriers, possibly explaining why dense pine forests survived in these areas. Additionally, much of the pine in the border lakes grew on isolated, protected islands, of which there are many thousands.[8]

White settlement fundamentally altered the fire regime and the landscape of the BWCAW, leading more forest fires to cover today than in the past. Logging and subsequent fires established aspen forests across most of the northland. Fire-dependent species like jack pine failed to regenerate; as they toppled, they were replaced by hardwoods. Fire suppression efforts and pulpwood logging not only froze the flora at this phase but also had a profound impact on the fauna of the area.

The animals that live in the forests today differ from those that did previously: eagles, osprey, caribou, elk, moose, cougar, Canada lynx, wolverine, and pileated woodpecker—species requiring late-stage forests—are now either completely extirpated or rare. Caribou and elk grazed the mosses and grasses in the open areas below the pine canopy. Moose were more common than deer before logging. Wolves, cougars, Canada lynx, and wolverines reigned at the top of the food chain, and black and carnivorous brown bear roamed Minnesota. Now there are no caribou, elk, brown bear, or wolverine. The fur trade, which wound down in the 1850s, almost wiped out many of the furbearers like otter, beaver, fisher, and pine martin, and habitat destruction by logging beginning in the 1880s stalled their recovery.

White-tailed deer were once rather rare in the north country. But since the creation of Superior National Forest in 1909, foresters, under pressure from hunting organizations, have been actively managing habitat for the species, and today deer herds have reached unprecedented numbers. Before 1920 there were about 480 caribou, 480 moose, 240 white-tailed deer, and 120 elk in the 344-square-mile Voyageurs National Park, twenty miles west of the BWCAW. By 1981 the caribou and elk were completely exterminated and the moose population had withered to just twenty-four animals due to hunting pressure and loss of habitat from logging. The deer population, on the other hand, had exploded to 1,200, more than the combined number of elk, caribou, and moose of prelogging days.

Recent efforts to reintroduce elk and caribou to the northland have failed, but wolf numbers are rising due to federal protection and the unnaturally high white-tailed deer populations. Moose populations remain low and unstable due in part to a brain worm that deer carry unharmed but that is fatal to moose. Canada lynx are beginning to return, and cougars have been re-established, but wolverines are completely extirpated. There is limited trapping of fishers and beaver again, but pine martin are still scarce. Today logging maintains habitats for deer and ruffed grouse, another previously rare species, over most of northern Minnesota save Voyageurs National Park and the BWCAW. Without logging, the populations of grouse and deer would decline but the numbers of moose, lynx, caribou, elk, pine martin, bear, wolverine, eagle, osprey, hawk, and a host of other old-growth-dependent species would increase.[9]

While logging and its aftermath changed the vegetation and wildlife of the border lakes region, the landscape itself was further altered by mere ideas. One of the most striking physical features of the United States, especially when viewed from an airplane, is the checkerboard look of it. The administrative necessities of land ownership, a western concept unknown before whites arrived, has changed the physical appearance of the landscape almost as much as the uses to which Americans have put the land. As settlers took control of new territory, they first laid ownership claims, describing the land so it could be captured in minute accuracy on a two-dimensional sheet of paper, saved in a cabinet or journal, registered, mortgaged, taxed, sold, and defended against other claims.

Thomas Jefferson proposed the system used to survey the public domain on May 7, 1784, and Congress adopted it a year later. Jefferson divided land into townships, a square six miles on each side or thirty-six square miles, about 23,760 acres. These squares he further divided into sections, quarter sections, acres, quarter acres, and so on down to inches, so that any spot in the United States can be accurately described and represented on paper without the need of map or picture.

Congress established the General Land Office in 1812 as a bureau to the U.S. Treasury Department. The GLO conducted public land surveys and provided for the distribution and management of the public domain, most notably the newly acquired environs of Jefferson's Louisiana Purchase. This land passed from public domain to private property in many ways. Lumbermen cut much of the Winton watershed without formality of ownership, but those who intended to save tracts for a later date used either homestead or preemption claims to tie up the land until they could cut it.

The Preemption Law, one of many enacted to encourage rapid settlement of the continent, allowed nontribal people who lived on land before it was part of the United States—people who had gone out beyond the borders of the young nation—the first chance at a parcel once it was surveyed. In Duluth, early missionaries and traders often used preemptive claims to gain ownership. The preemptor had to file a declaratory statement within three months of the local land office's receipt of the survey plat or within three months of making settlement. When the GLO announced, with ads in the appropriate papers, the auction of a section, the preemptor paid $1.25 per acre for the land or risked losing it to the highest bidder. A preemptive claim took precedence over all others.

A second significant land law was the Homestead Act of 1862. Republican president Abraham Lincoln, in the spirit of Jefferson's ideal of

a landed agrarian utopia and seeking a practical way to boost an economically fragile Union during the war, invited farmers to claim any
unoccupied, surveyed land, clear it, and farm it. So began the most ex-
pansive and expensive social welfare program in history, during which
one-eighth of the public domain passed into private ownership. The
price for 160 acres was settling it: building a twelve-by-twelve-foot
home (with windows), raising crops and animals, and living there for
five years. Millions surged into Indiana and Illinois and then across the
Mississippi River into Iowa and Kansas, into the regions that would become Nebraska, the Dakotas, and Colorado, and out to the farthest corners of the country.[10]

But in northern Minnesota there was little soil and only a seventy-
day growing season, and predators and severe weather were hard on
livestock. The unwise who tried their luck at farming were mostly un-
successful. In this region, the Homestead Law was shamefully abused:
less than ten percent of the homesteads on the Arrowhead were legitimate. Farmers did not emigrate to the border lakes; loggers did. As each
citizen was allowed only one homestead in his or her lifetime, lumbermen typically paid dummy homesteaders one hundred dollars each to
transfer their homestead title to the lumber company.[11]

This was not the only abuse in the northern forest. Frontier towns,
like Winton and Ely, desired settlement, progress, and development,
and the few meager protective measures enacted were not enforced.
Land law abuses continued defiantly across the Arrowhead, whose settlers welcomed the economic vitality brought by the logging industry.
But Easterners, looking at their sprawling cities and cutover lands,
readily understood the true costs of forest devastation. They saw real
benefits in a program of restricted, reasonable, and sustainable harvesting of trees: conservation. Prompted by their frontier constituen-
cies, Western legislators initially blocked most such legislation. But on
January 9, 1891, special agents of the Duluth Land Office John Brown
and Ronald Keegan reported that 50 million board feet of logs, worth
over $1 million, had been stolen. This unconscionable theft and con-
tinued destruction—especially from the uncontrolled wildfires that
swept the newly cleared land—finally forced government controls.[12]

On March 3, 1891, Congress repealed the Preemption Law and revised the Homestead Act. According to the changes, "bona fide settlers" like miners and farmers could remove timber from their lands before they held title, but they were forbidden to sell this timber or transfer their claim on the land. Congress also altered the Homestead Act's commutation clause, which allowed settlers to pay $1.25 per acre in lieu of living on a claim for five years, increasing the waiting period from six months to fourteen. After the repeal of the Preemption Law, land speculators used the commutation clause to gather pinelands. From July 1, 1899, to June 30, 1903, 89 percent of the commuted entries were transferred to other owners, most likely speculators, usually on the day or the day after they were filed. In 1892, the year after the repeal of the

*Cutover tangles of slash left in logging's wake*
*led to inevitable wildfires that destroyed the few trees spared from the ax.*

Preemption Law, entry men filed on 241,095 acres at the Duluth Land Office. By 1901 that number had risen to three hundred thousand acres. Theft under the new law was only slightly less convenient than it had been under the old, and enforcement no more rigorous.[13]

On April 23, 1893, a Minnesota Senate investigating committee published the results of its inquiry into timber depredations in the state. The charges included bribery, theft, larceny, perjury, fraud, and arson. Lumbermen filed false preemption entries, bribed surveyors and state scalers to falsify board-foot estimates, intimidated legal patent-holders into selling, rigged land auctions through pre-agreed bidding, and stole millions of trees outright. None of these offences, however, was the major insult to posterity. The committee wrote:

> This evidence establishes . . . that the State of Minnesota has been robbed of millions of dollars worth of its property during the past fifteen years and that the most gigantic fraud has been practiced upon the school fund, a fund which every good citizen has hoped to see preserved undiminished for the benefit of the present generation and posterity.

The federal government granted sections six and thirty-six from each township to the states, intending these lands and their resources to fund schools. But these "school sections" were easier pickings for the timber thieves because there was no chance of running across any other developer with a legitimate claim on the land. By 1900 Minnesota had received only $7 million for its school lands, while the value of the timber cut in Minnesota from 1840 to 1932 was nearly $1.7 billion. Today the state's schools are funded by property taxes, a direct result of the theft of school timber resources a century ago. Ignatius Donnelly, future lieutenant governor, U.S. representative, and People's candidate for governor, wrote in the final report of the investigating committee:

> What then should be said of the "Stumpage Thieves," whose profession, whose every instinct is child robbery, and to whom falsehood is a stimulant and perjury a pastime? They should never be allowed to pass into oblivion; our children and our children's children should be taught the enormity of their crime, and their

reputation should never be allowed to be galvanized into seeming respectability by an outward show of virtue and piety, or pretensions of benevolence.[14]

These outrageous acts and others like them finally forced reform. As logging operations were getting up to speed in the border lakes region, the freewheeling style of land acquisition that had been the rule in the United States was changing. The Winton watershed would be the first harvest under the new banner of forestry. Gifford Pinchot and Theodore Roosevelt promoted a rational public domain policy to replace the lawless bedlam of the pioneering days. Conservationists promised that scientific, rational removal of wood could provide a sustained yield without destroying the resource, the forest. Science was to rule, not commerce. By the time conservation became national policy, a practical lumberman from Muskoka, Ontario, Robert Whiteside, was already working in the border lakes. Whiteside, one of the last American pioneers, was the vanguard in the final cut of eastern white pine. But Whiteside's concerns were logistical, not philosophical or scientific. It was his notions, and those of other timber men like him, that would shape the border lakes as the local Ojibwe gave way, ending the traditional fire regimes that had ruled for centuries.

# 2

## Pioneer Lumbering

*I'm going to America*
*Everyone is on his way*
*The American shores are sanded*
*with gold they say.*
*I'll embark from Cork*
*on a small boat and go*
*'cause Ireland can't support*
*the children of her poor.*

---

THE SUMMER OF 1846 was the second warmest of the nineteenth century. July, August, and September had more than sixty-four days of rain. The Irish sky imposed upon the earth, leaden gray and low hung, the air moist and warm and heavy and diseased. These combined conditions created the perfect habitat for a newly arrived Peruvian potato blight, *Phytophthora infestans*, to which the one species of potato grown in Ireland was very susceptible. The entire crop failed, and more than one million people died in Black '47 or *An Gorta Mor*, the famine that followed. Ireland, the most densely populated area of Europe at the time, saw its population drop from eight million to five million. Almost two million fled starvation, choosing instead the dangers of a typhus-, dysentery-, dropsy-, and scurvy-ridden Atlantic crossing.

Robert Whiteside's parents and three of his siblings joined this diaspora. Eventually they settled in Muskoka, Ontario, where the family soon numbered six boys and three girls. Robert Whiteside worked his way up from the bottom of the lumber trade, saving his pay through thrift and sensible living. He bought a fine team of horses and hired himself out as a teamster. As the 1870s closed and the logging industry around Muskoka collapsed, Robert and his brothers pulled stumps to clear the land for farms, but in 1880, as even this work faded, Robert decided to go after virgin stands elsewhere. At age twenty-five, with thirty-five hundred dollars in his pocket and several fine teams of logging horses, he moved to Duluth, Minnesota.

This relocation initially proved unlucky. Robert contracted to build a dam, but expenses overran profits and he lost fifteen hundred dollars. The following winter he took on a logging contract, but again he lost. In spring 1881 he sold his horses and satisfied his debts with four dollars to spare. The next winter he worked for Hall and Norton as logging foreman at a camp on the Black River in Wisconsin, but that spring Whiteside outfitted in Duluth and walked into the wilderness of northern Minnesota to look for unclaimed pinelands. His timing could not have been better. His luck was about to change.[1]

George Stuntz, a surveyor who had been in the northland three decades, and Bob Stone, a Yankee Iowan banker ruined in the war, had been trying for years to open what would become the richest iron ore mine in the world ninety miles north of Duluth. Finally they had convinced Charlemagne Tower, an eastern financier, to sink $3 million into the district. Crews were busy building railroads, shipping docks, stores, warehouses, boarding houses, and all manner of engine sheds, shops, and stables stretching along the right of way from Two Harbors to the ore outcroppings. Men were erecting the new towns of Tower and Soudan on the shores of Lake Vermilion, and Cornish deep drift miners were stockpiling the rifle-barrel-blue hematite for eventual shipment via the railroad. Others were installing enormous elevators to unload the ore, roundhouses to turn the engines, and further infrastructure to support the operations.

In a land where the rivers run north, away from any market or milling center, these improvements were critical to the success of Whiteside's vision. Lumbering alone could not generate enough cash to justify such expenditures, but once the trains were built lumbermen could afford to pay freight to ship dried boards to the Great Lakes and then to eastern markets. Whiteside explored north, west, and east of Tower's mining operations. Alone, he traipsed over rocky ridges and sphagnum swamps, through black spruce stands and cedar bogs. Summers, he suffered mosquitoes and black flies; winters, when traveling was easier, temperatures fell far below zero. He walked beside rivers, noting the best sites for dams and sluiceways, and studied the prevailing winds in anticipation of floating logs across lakes. He sketched possible logging roads and rail extensions on his maps and marked the locations of waterfalls suitable for generating power to run future mills.

Whiteside searched for elements he could parlay into a logging enterprise. Most important, of course, the trees had to be prime. But they also needed to be accessible, located next to a lake or river deep enough to float them to a mill. Whiteside knew the best way to control the pine in any area was to control the watershed, the means of transport. He made himself familiar with the Winton watershed, a complex maze of interconnected lakes, muskeg, and rivers, a place where islands and the mainland are often indistinguishable.

After surveying the myriad rivers, lakes, and flowages, Robert Whiteside chose Fall Lake as the prime base for milling operations and the Stony River drainage to furnish the pine. More than 400 million board feet of timber were directly accessible by water to the north of Fall Lake, and another 500 million board feet of prime-grade white pine could easily be floated in from the south. Including the pine that would be accessible with improvements, the figures rose into the billions. Fall Lake is twenty miles north and east of Tower, in the heart of the rugged border lakes, what would become the BWCAW. The lake adjoined all the timber on Birch Lake and the Roaring Stony River south for fifty miles to the headwaters of the Winton watershed at Source Lake, high on the north slope of the Laurentian Divide. Looking north, however, Fall Lake is so situated that with short portages between lakes and rivers it connects to timberlands spreading twenty miles past Fourtown and Horse Lakes, east to Knife Lake, and west almost to the Rainy Lake system. Whiteside had chosen well indeed.[2]

After locating the pine, Robert Whiteside encouraged his brothers-in-law Edward Robinson and John Densmore and brothers Richard,

Job, John, and James to join him in Duluth. Together they traveled north to secure homesteads beyond the edge of land either civilized or surveyed. The land office was about to open the township containing Fall Lake, and Robert Whiteside intended to lock up logging operations on the Winton watershed, the last stands of eastern white pine in the country. Their destination was a strip of land between Shagawa and Burntside Lakes. A marvelous tract of white pine grew on the south shore of Shagawa, trees like the brothers had known in their youth. Once there, they erected a shanty and with a transit, compass, and survey chain measured off and blazed the boundaries of a 160-acre tract. They claimed more monolithic pine on land that would become downtown Ely. At the east end of Shagawa and Fall Lakes they set more claims. And when they were done, they beat their way back toward Duluth and the U.S. Land Office for the opening of the section.[3]

On the trail just outside the muddy turmoil of Tower, the party ran into a group of men headed north. Two brothers, Martin and William Pattison, were after iron, not timber. Having studied the Lake Vermilion iron formation, they believed those outcroppings to be only one place where iron ore broke through the Laurentian shield. Geological contours led them to Shagawa Lake, where on the southeast corner they discovered a small surface outcropping. But the Pattison brothers also encountered the blaze marks and homestead shanties left by Robert Whiteside. Six months elapsed before the Pattisons could contact him about his claim, and during that time Whiteside placed over sixty dummy homestead claims, gaining control of nearly ten thousand acres of prime timberland.

Captain H. R. Harvey, Civil War veteran and mining expert, discovered more ore on another of Whiteside's claims. Thus, while securing some of the finest eastern white pine stands left in the world, Whiteside had inadvertently claimed some of the most valuable mining lands as well, including the future sites of the Chandler, Pioneer, Zenith, and Sibley iron mines. Before he realized the value of the minerals, however, Whiteside sold the Chandler claim for two thousand dollars and the Sibley for fifteen hundred. Even so, his interest in the Pioneer and Zenith mines made him the richest man in the state for many years.[4]

A full six years after Whiteside moved to Duluth and began his explorations, the *Vermilion Iron Journal* reported on October 20, 1887:

> The town of Ely is coming to the front but not very much. [No more] building will be done there until next winter when timber will be hauled from Tower on the ice or over this new road on the snow. The lumber at present is worth $40.00 per thousand at Ely, it all being cut with whipsaws. There is a portable sawmill there, but the mining company owns it and consumes the entire output themselves.

In 1887 and 1888 the Whiteside brothers cut ties for the new railroad extension from Tower to Ely and built bunkhouses for the five to six hundred Scandinavian workers who came in on the Duluth and Iron Range Railroad. The Whitesides hauled lumber over the winter road from Tower and opened the Pioneer Hotel, Ely's first boarding house and restaurant, which younger brother Job managed. Soon an advertisement ran in the *Journal:* "The new town of Ely will be the town of the great Vermilion Iron Range and Whiteside's Addition will be the finest part of it." Whiteside's Park is a remnant of early city planning by the old logger.[5]

Also that fall, the *Journal* reported that lumbermen from Michigan, the Mee brothers and Doctor Mead, had bought large tracts of pine near Shagawa Lake from Robert Whiteside. The story noted: "A sawmill is to be built at once . . . and timber cut for both mines and dwellings." But Whiteside was slow to forget his early failures and did not jump into competition with the Mees. Logging is a risky business, not only brutal and dangerous work for the lumberjack but also fraught with uncertainty for the owner. Before investors realize any profit they must build a sawmill and roads, buy tugs and barges, build and outfit camps, feed hundreds of hungry jacks and horses through long winters, get the heavy logs from forest to mill, and fill orders from eastern markets, altogether a huge capital investment. Frequent forest fires and mill fires could destroy a year's inventory in a day. Too much snow made logging difficult or even impossible, while in dry years logs could be stranded in the woods or at landings miles from the mill.

But the shrewd Whiteside knew the increasing scarcity of pine logs insured his eventual success without risk. As the last pine fell in more accessible districts, the value of Whiteside's trees rose steadily. In 1891, the boosters at the *Vermilion Iron Journal* office noted: "The census will report [that] there is more standing pine in Minnesota than in Michigan or Wisconsin." It was only a matter of time before the logging industry relocated to the northwest, along the border lakes.[6]

The Whiteside brothers continued to do some contract logging along the rail line from Tower to Ely on Armstrong and Robinson Lakes, and they sold a few pine logs to the sawmill on East Two River in Tower. But mostly they waited for a buyer for their lands in the border lakes. The first serious offer came from Samuel G. Knox. As the Wisconsin pineries expired, Knox sent his future grandson-in-law, Billy Winton, north to locate pinelands. Billy quickly realized that Whiteside held the most important tracts, and he urged Knox to travel to Duluth and negotiate a sale.

From Union Depot Knox viewed Lake Superior to the south and east. Steep hills to the northwest crowded Duluth's ten blocks of commercial district on the flats against the lake. The Longsdale Building, a red brownstone, squatted heavy and ornate on a shoulder of the hill, and on the seventh floor Knox found Robert Whiteside's offices, a two-room suite more modest than the owner's reputation. Whiteside described the immense pineries that lay just north, east, and south of Ely. He told Knox about a peninsula on the south shore of Fall Lake, the perfect location for a sawmill. Fall Lake was seven miles long and surrounded by majestic pinelands. Two rivers, the Kawishiwi and the Shagawa, flowed into it, both connecting to other chains of lakes and rivers, linking hundreds of thousands of acres of timber. While much of the pine this far north did not compare in quality to the trees that Knox had cut in Wisconsin, these stands were the last in the northland. Later that week Knox purchased eighty acres on the southwest end of Fall Lake.

The *Ely Times* kept close watch on the developments. On January 12, 1893, Knox, Winton, and F. D. Smith incorporated the Northern Lumber Company, which, despite official documentation, was forever known as Knox Lumber Company. Robert Whiteside served as a contract logger and general bookkeeper for the firm. In one year's time Whiteside and Knox built a three-mile wagon road extension from Ely to Fall Lake, a sawmill, logging camps large enough to support hundreds of men, barns, stables, warehouses, offices, a train station, and housing for the sawmill crew. Knox named the new town Winton, after Billy.

In October 1893 work began on a Duluth and Iron Range Railroad extension from Ely to Knox mill. Also that October, Richard Whiteside fashioned a special crib to lift the steamship *Paul* out of Shagawa Lake and with a team of eight horses hauled the boat up Finn Hill to Chapman Street, north out of town, and over the newly cleared road to Fall Lake. As soon as the *Paul* splashed into the lake it began to transport men and supplies to the north end, where they worked to build more camps before the snow fell.

By the end of November 1893, there were no fewer than five camps landing logs for the first season's cut. Most were along the rail line from Tower in the Robinson, Armstrong, and Eagles Nest Lakes area. Besides those on the north shore of Fall Lake, there were camps on Farm Lake. The Whitesides expected to have 15 million board feet of logs banked by spring breakup.

The new Duluth and Iron Range extension reached the mill in late December, and the millwright spent the rest of the winter building the mill. His job was critical because once the logs started coming any shutdown would hamper not only company profits but also the livelihood of most of the town's population. The summer run was the climax of the work of many men: Whiteside, who years before had located the pine, the agents and lawyers who had secured rights to the trees, the lumberjacks and river pigs who had felled and coaxed those trees across miles of wilderness to the mill, and the salesmen who had sold the boards those trees would produce even while they were still swaying gently on their stumps. The millwright was the key to the entire sequence.

On March 3, 1894, the Knox Lumber Company mill whistle echoed through Winton, the first throb of the town's shrill heartbeat. For the next thirty years the whistle marked weddings, funerals, fires, and baseball victories. The Knox mill stood three stories tall beside Fall Lake. On the top floor was a filing or swaging shop, where men repaired saw

*Working on South Farm Lake in 1928,*
*a jack maneuvers a log with a short-handled cant hook.*

blades, adjusted the angle of the saw teeth, and ground those teeth to a razor edge.

Production took place on the second floor, where the bull chain led from the millpond up to the second story landing. Out in the water men kept logs feeding toward this chain with peavey poles, named for blacksmith Joseph Peavey of Stillwater, Maine, who designed the tool in 1858. A twenty-foot handle led to a pointed tip with a hinged hook that also came to a sharp point. By pushing the point into a log and setting the hook, a pond man could get enough leverage to move the largest specimens, even when balanced on another bobbing log. The long peavey also kept men who fell into the water from slipping between the logs. It was nearly impossible for a jack to pull himself out of a crowded millpond and back onto the rolling logs without help. The long peavey saved many men from drowning.

The pond men set the bull chain's spiked hooks into the logs, small end first. Two other spiked hooks sixteen feet down the chain held the wide ends. As the logs traveled up the bull chain a series of high-pressure water jets washed off dirt or gravel that would damage the saws. On the second floor men disengaged the logs from the chain and stacked them above the sliding sawmill carriage using cant dogs, short-handled peaveys with toe rings and lips instead of spikes at the end. Usually two or four men worked this deck, two disengaging the logs from the bull chain and two feeding the waiting logs onto the carriage.

Once they were loaded on the carriage the sawyer made as many square boards from the round logs as possible, cutting to avoid sap stain or knots, viewing the raw logs as two-by-fours, four-by-fours, lath, sash, or plank. He had to know the orders for the company: it did no good to cut stacks of beautiful planks if Knox was trying to fill a structural timber contract. The sawyer controlled the back and forth motion of the log carriage, but it was the setter, riding the carriage, who actually positioned the log before each cut. The setter ran machinery that jacked the log from one side to the other and set it the correct distance from the saw so that a sawyer could make a uniform board of any dimension. Because all of this happened in the deafening roar of a running sawmill, the sawyer communicated his instructions to the setter with hand signals.

The sawyer worked in a cage set into the floor beside the spinning saw. A high plank fence reinforced with cast iron shielded him if a saw blade broke. Sawyers had to be virtually ambidextrous, both hands working the levers of the steam feed and signaling to the setter, both feet pressing carriage and saw controls on the floor. Once the sawyer had squared up a log, he sent it through a gang saw. As the name implies, the saw had many blades, all of them adjustable so that one log could be cut into a number of boards of a given dimension.

*Green line workers at the Skibo Timber Company process slag—the round edges of logs—around 1913.*

From there the boards slid along a preset guide into the edger, a saw with at least two blades and sometimes many more. Rollers pulled the plank through the teeth, holding it in place from both above and below while the saw trimmed it to the appropriate dimension. In some cases, where there were multiple pairs of saws at work in the edger, a single plank might be fed in and many smaller dimension pieces, like two-by-fours or even smaller, would emerge from the other end. The last saw on the second floor was the end cut, positioned at the top of the gang-way leading to the first floor and the green line. This saw was also adjustable, but instead of being fed in end first, boards traveled through sideways and were trimmed to an exact length.

Next, the boards slid down the green line, to where a worker's only required asset was a strong back. The skilled worker, the grader, sorted boards according to a qualitative scale, while others, usually new men, stacked lumber on two-wheeled wagons, the ends of the boards trailing on the ground. The lumberyard's thick plank roads protected the fresh boards, which the men were very careful to keep clean. Once bundled and transported to their spot in the drying yard, the boards were stacked. The stackers worked in pairs, one man tipping up the board to another who lifted it the rest of the way to the top. They placed spacers at each level so that circulating air dried the boards. They built the piles with a slight slant to drain rainwater or snow melt. Slivers from the rough-cut and unplaned lumber quickly turned cotton or even wool clothing into rags, so stackers wore leather aprons and heavy gloves to protect their clothing and hands.

An amazing enterprise, the Knox lumberyard was at one point almost a mile long, its lumber piles stacked twenty or even thirty feet high. At any given time many million feet of lumber might be on hand, all of it at various stages of drying, enough to build a small city. As the orders came in, the office communicated what types of lumber were needed that day, week, or month to the yard foreman, whose men disassembled the correct pile and loaded it onto cars that traveled on a rail line through the center of the yard. As an added precaution against dirtying the fresh lumber, stackers wore felt-soled shoes. Their task required speed and agility: they were usually paid by the piece moved, and they often worked through the night to fill an order.

If the order called for planed lumber, the foreman transferred boards to the planing mill, located at the end of the yard some distance from the main operation. On one side, piled lumber awaited the shavers, and on the other, a platform led directly to rail cars so the finished lumber would not have to sit outside where it might get dirty. The planer was an exact device, with cuts measured in small fractions of inches. Steel

*Teamster Charlie Provost, stackers Otto Avaskainen and Ben Antelson, and scaler Chris Garson pose in the St. Croix mill drying yard around 1912. The horses' elaborate harnesses protected them from flies.*

drums fitted with blades spun at high speed to shave off just enough wood to fit the order's specifications. After a board emerged from the planer it was smooth and clean, requiring nothing but a little paint or varnish. The planers claimed that while a meticulous carpenter might pass a piece of sandpaper over their boards, he did so mostly for show.

Even in a milling operation of this size, nothing was wasted. At each saw the scraps fell through hoppers onto a conveyor and large fans blew sawdust through a three-foot-wide pipe. This refuse fired the furnace, which raised steam to run the mill machinery.

The week after the mill opened, Knox outfitted it with steam-powered turbines to generate electrical current, installed electric lights, hired more workers, and ran the mill through the night as well. The loggers kept pace, banking 11 million feet of logs at Fall Lake and hauling in additional logs by rail. That first summer was not without its setbacks, however. Foreman George Brown caught his coat in the machinery and was dragged into the gears; Dr. Shipman had to amputate Brown's mangled arm. Interim mill manager John Whiteside had some trouble controlling the water levels on Fall Lake: by May the water had risen six inches above the mill's floor, briefly shutting down operations. Then, on July 27, a forest fire burned the new store, the office, and luggage belonging to Mr. and Mrs. Knox, who had just arrived by train. The damage from the fire was estimated at sixteen hundred dollars. Despite these impediments, John Whiteside and the seventy men in his employ still turned out about one hundred thousand board feet daily. While some of the lumber went to build Ely and Winton, a daily shipment of about eighteen carloads of sawn wood traveled down the Duluth and Iron Range line to Two Harbors and from there to the East Coast.

The next year saw many improvements in the mill. John Whiteside ordered four new boilers, sixteen feet tall with sixteen-inch-thick steel walls, from the Otis Company of Indianapolis, Indiana, to power new Lytle engines built by Indianapolis's Commercial Electric Company. He lit every dark corner of the mill, the green line, the lumber drying yards, and the railroad loading docks. He set up a shingle department on the first floor of the mill that produced about twenty-five thousand shingles daily. He refit the second floor to hold a 45-foot band saw and discarded the circular saw. He installed spurs off the railroad line to transport logs in winter. To feed this voracious mill, the Knox Company purchased 70 million board feet of white pine stumpage—at $2.50 per thousand feet—from lumberman J. J. Rupp of Saginaw, Michigan, in the Farm Lake and Kawishiwi River area. Later that fall, Knox acquired scattered pinelands south of Robinson and Eagles Nest Lakes from lumbermen in Grand Rapids, Michigan.

Altogether the Knox Company had more than four hundred men working to supply the mill with logs that year. The Whitesides continued logging their tracts: Robert cut at milepost 108 on the rail line just south of Wolf Lake; Job built a camp on Garden Lake; Richard spent another winter on the Kawishiwi; and John Densmore built a camp four miles south of Winton in the White Iron Lake area. While most of their cut went to Knox, the Whitesides still sold logs to Howe Lumber Company in Tower and the mines in both Tower and Ely.

On November 7, 1895, temperatures dropped and Fall Lake froze. Because the only feasible means of moving logs up to the second-floor sawing room was to float them onto the bull chain, a frozen millpond meant the saws would be silent until spring thaw. The Knox Lumber Company mill closed for the season, having cut more than 20 million board feet that year. But John Whiteside soon devised a way reopen by running extra pipes off the Otis boilers and into Fall Lake to heat the water. He extended the rail spur into the lake and dumped logs directly off the trestle into the steaming pond. By Christmas, the whistle blew and Knox mill reopened. During January 1896, the mill received 257 cars of logs from Robinson Lake, 176 cars from Robert Whiteside, and about 11 cars from John Densmore's camp. That winter the mill produced about eighty thousand board feet each day.

A year later, Knox continued to expand his operations, inviting a group of engineers to survey Kawishiwi Falls. Their efforts were reported in the March 11, 1898, *Ely Miner:* "Work at [Kawishiwi] falls is progressing rapidly and soon the picturesqueness of this beautiful place will be eliminated. The rocks are being blasted so as to facilitate the driving of logs."

While the mill in 1898 cut a respectable 16 million board feet, Knox planned to double its output. John Whiteside installed another 45-foot band saw, more new engines, and an additional battery of boilers. But as the only large-scale lumber company north of Tower, Knox could not come close to clearing all of the border lakes' timberlands. As pine in other parts of the state became more difficult to find, lumbermen began to look north for supply. Knox may have gotten a head start, but in September 1898, genial Irishman Robert Whiteside brought in new competition, selling a mill site just down from Knox's operation on Fall Lake to the Swallow and Hopkins Lumber Company.

# 3

## The Cut Increases

*About the old times. Say, them old time tales where we greased the skids and rode the oxen and all that noise? Them oldtime jacks in mustaches and ten-gallon hats carryin' a misery whip over their shoulder lookin' all dashing and romantic . . . they weren't the ones! that really rolled the logs. No. No sir. It was boys . . . what had the sense to get hold of a machine. . . .*

*The trucks! The cats! The yarders! I say more power to 'em. . . . There weren't nothin' good about the good old days . . . didn't even make a dent in the shade. You need to get in there with some machines an' tear hell out of it!*

KEN KESEY, *Sometimes a Great Notion*

LOUIS HOPKINS was a regular at Duluth Land Office auctions, a familiar face at the registrar's, an astute, affable, and aggressive collector of pine tracts north of Ely, as far west as Lake Vermilion and east almost to Knife Lake. Financier George Swallow was from Wilmette, Illinois, an affluent suburb north of Chicago. These two men would be responsible for plucking about a billion board feet of old pine tracts from the heart of what is now the BWCAW. Hopkins had been in the northland collecting pine stumpage for years. By 1898 the value of the stands he had amassed justified Swallow's capital investment to harvest the trees, mill them, and ship the boards to market. The two formed Swallow and Hopkins Lumber Company.[1]

Swallow and Hopkins contracted with Cross Lake Logging to log and mill their trees. Incorporated in 1890, the Cross Lake company was perhaps the busiest lumberjack crew in Minnesota then, cutting for Weyerhaeuser, Hall and Ducey, Bovey-De Laittre, and the Itasca Lumber Company. But with Swallow and Hopkins's trees, located on slightly more than two hundred thousand acres of Minnesota's roughest country, Sam Simpson, owner of Cross Lake along with partners E. C. Whitney and John L. McGuire, faced greater logistical problems than had the Knox Company.[2]

The border lakes pose remarkable transportation challenges. Much of the area is water, but the lakes and rivers are broken by steep ridges and myriad islands and swamps. Robert Whiteside had chosen the most easily accessible stands, to the south, mostly along the Kawishiwi and Stony Rivers, but Swallow and Hopkins's trees were north, downstream from Fall Lake, amongst the maze of lakes and streams that meandered northeast to Hudson Bay. Because their trees were some of the most remote in the entire United States, their logging operations had to be extremely innovative, utilizing almost every conceivable mode of transportation available at the time.[3]

Simpson rose to the challenge, agreeing to cut 50 million board feet of timber off Swallow and Hopkins's pine tracts, build Swallow and Hopkins a mill, saw the logs, and deliver finished lumber for shipment the following spring. An announcement of the new mill made the front page of the September 28, 1898, issue of the *Ely Miner,* which carefully reported every decision the company made in the coming years. Simpson leased a site on Fall Lake from Robert Whiteside, oversaw construction of a mill, and contracted for a new Duluth and Iron Range Railroad spur to connect his operation to the main line. Initially, he avoided the difficult transportation problems Swallow and Hopkins's holdings posed by collecting logs from along the Duluth and Iron Range route or upstream from the Burntside or Birch Lake waterways, building two camps on Burntside Lake and logging the most accessible stands on Fall Lake.[4]

In early February 1899, Diamond Iron Works of Minneapolis shipped a new 600-horsepower steam engine, an automatic log feed, and a single-sided band saw directly to the Swallow and Hopkins sawmill on the new Duluth and Iron Range extension. By the time the ice went out, Good and Russell expected to have about 16 million board feet banked from their six camps, and Good intended to have the mill running by April 15.[5]

With Simpson handling the construction of the infrastructure, the company turned to staffing their office, camps, and mill. Swallow and Hopkins hired George "Herb" Good, a young businessman with logging experience, as an in-house bookkeeper, moving him into its new offices in Winton. An old ally of Simpson's, Mr. McTiver, arrived early that fall from Wisconsin's defunct pineries to put in a fifty-man camp upstream on White Iron Lake. He and his men cut hard through the winter, and early in May they rode the spring freshets to Fall Lake with seven million board feet of logs for Simpson's boom. McTiver returned to Sheboygan, Wisconsin, for the summer, but like a migratory bird, his instincts running in reverse, he made his way north in fall 1899 to run Simpson's camps on Ella Hall Lake.[6]

On June 21, 1899, Simpson returned from Minneapolis with a trained crew and started up the mill with his employers Louis Hopkins and George Swallow on hand to witness its grand opening. Swallow and Hopkins next hired J. C. Russell as the company's office manager and bookkeeper; Good, at age twenty-three, became general superintendent. Good enjoyed success behind a desk, but he made his biggest contributions in the woods, uncannily moving thousands of logs miles upstream through rugged wilderness. Good solved many of the problems Simpson had forestalled.[7]

In winter 1899, Good built three camps, running one on Fall Lake with W. Ingram while "One-armed Sullivan" operated another on Mud Lake and Pat McAlpine a third on Ella Hall Lake. Good's three camps harvested about 15 million board feet of logs that first year. To move those logs to Fall Lake, Good built a small, temporary railroad to the other two camps, employing hoists to load the logs onto russell cars. Consisting of flat cribs equipped with wheels, russells were tough, inexpensive, stripped-down workhorses built for the north woods. Good brought the cars in from Two Harbors just in time for the first season's run, choosing a durable little Lima Shay Locomotive known as the Three Spot to pull the russells on his line.[8]

Ever the innovator, Good soon found ways to improve the russells. Top loaders typically used corner bind chains to hold the outside logs in place and wrapper chains to fasten the load to the car. Good and mechanical engineer Al Cross added automatic car stakes, mechanical arms that held the logs during transport, making binding chains obsolete. At the Fall Lake end of the line, the rails ran out over the water on a dead-end trestle, and a flip of a lever lowered the arms, dumping the load into the lake and sending up massive sheets of spray. From there the jacks boomed the logs and towed them to the millpond. Good's innovation was not only safer, it was also much faster, saving men from having to bind and unbind the loads with chain.[9]

Like Knox, Swallow and Hopkins sold most of its lumber to Eastern dealers. High-grade lumber can only be made from old-growth pine, trees whose grain is tight from growing slowly, lacking knot or burl because lower branches have withered from lack of light. The East Coast, cleared of its old pine a century earlier, had to import its choice lumber, and this was the main market the Winton mills served. In 1900, its first full year of operations, during which total sales were two hundred fifty thousand dollars, Swallow and Hopkins's entire output of "number two" and better boards shipped down the lakes either by freighter to Tonawanda, New York, near Niagara Falls, or by rail to Chicago. The company sent its lower grades of lumber west to the treeless Great Plains.[10]

When Simpson returned to Cross Lake Lumber Company to take on other contracts, Good took charge of the Swallow and Hopkins operation. Knowing that he would be unable to rely on independent timber suppliers and loggers like the Whitesides, whose sources of trees were rapidly dwindling, Good faced a challenge for the next season: harvesting the timber to the north, downstream from the mill.[11]

As he investigated ways to reach Swallow and Hopkins's stands, Good considered land just east of Newton Lake up to Pipestone Bay, which Swallow had bought in December 1898 for $33,750. On this land, Good built a railroad paralleling the Newton Lake chain with a short spur about halfway up the line connecting to Newton Lake and another a bit farther north cutting off to the northeast, presumably to reach other valuable pine. That March, Good bought an old Shay Locomotive known as the Two Spot and began shuttling logs into Fall Lake, but the next year he abandoned the route as too difficult and spent his summer searching for a permanent line.[12]

Good described the route he chose:

Soon after we had used the Mud-Ella Hall railroad log haul satisfactorily we located a good railroad route from Fall Lake direct to Basswood. We followed a portion of the Mud Lake route and built the

*Earl West, Al Oaks, Herb Good, and Al Cross pose in front of a russell car equipped with their innovative mechanical stakes, which were far safer and more quickly operated than the old-fashioned method of wrapping chain around the load to hold it to the car.*

new railroad extension by way of Rice Lake on to Basswood. This we completed in 1901 after we completed the logging in the Mud-Ella Hall area. We abandoned that portion of the railroad we didn't need, using the rails for the new railroad.[13]

Swallow and Hopkins did not own all of this route, but as Good himself later admitted, "we never obtained any special right-of-way rights because in those days no one bothered with such things." Fire had burned the land some fifty or sixty years before, and a good stand of jack pine—a resinous tree resistant to rot and perfect for railroad ties—grew there. Local Ojibwe cut firewood to fuel the boilers, moved earth, laid rails. They drilled and blasted rock ledges and used the talus to fill low areas. Intending it to last for many seasons, Good's crew graded, graveled, and ballasted the line well. At four miles long, it became forever known as Fourmile Portage. Good's mill was now connected not only to the magnificent Basswood Lake pine but also to most of the border lakes, allowing him to move logs from the thousands of densely timbered islands and miles of lakeshores directly to the Swallow and Hopkins bull chain. The only bottleneck occurred at Basswood Lake, when the logs had to be lifted onto Good's modified russell cars.[14]

Two local Ojibwe men, John Linklater and Vincent Default, managed this dangerous and tricky work at what became known as Hoist Bay. At first they cross-hauled the heavy logs and swung them onto russells using gentle black-eyed Morgans for power and an overhead jammer, a tripod and pulley rig, for leverage. To mechanize this process and increase safety, Good fashioned a heavy, timbered incline with two sprockets about ten feet apart. A steam engine drove the sprocket, turning two endless chains with metal arms welded onto them that lifted logs from the water and rolled them up and into a waiting russell car, then turned over the top gear and traveled under the cribbing back to the water in an unremitting cycle. With this improvement, Linklater and Default fed a donkey engine boiler instead of their horses.[15]

The BWCAW is canoe country, as much water as land. Good's innovative railroads carried the logs over the land, but he contracted with William Jeffrey to move logs across the water. Jeffrey's first challenge was getting his steamships from Duluth harbor to the border lakes. The first to arrive was the steamship *Nellie J*, which Jeffrey drove from Duluth to Two Harbors and lifted to a flat car for the trip to the Fall Lake railhead. From there he steamed to Fourmile Portage, loaded the steamship onto a russell car for the trip over the portage, and launched it into Basswood Lake. Jeffrey soon brought other tugs up to the chain of lakes and ran all of Swallow and Hopkins's towing operations, supplying not only the boats, towing lines, boom men, engineers, and crew but any other equipment needed for water transport.

With Jeffrey's help, Good constructed a rail line in sections: his answer to the challenges presented by the border lakes. When the path

*Part of Swallow and Hopkins's towing fleet, the* Nellie J *and the* Meretie J, *at rest on Fall Lake.*

was interrupted by water, instead of erecting a series of trestles or bridges, Good's men built scows to ferry the railroad engines and cars over the water. Thirty feet wide and eighty feet long, with standard-gauge rails spiked into a rough plank deck, the scows were improbable in design but brilliant in function. Loaded with two russells, they rode low in the water behind the *Nellie J*, but—even as waves breached the deck and flooded the scows—they floated like wide, flat corks and did not capsize.

With these transportation questions answered, Good built the first and largest camp on Basswood Lake, on the south shore of Washington Island, near Sand Beach. Washington Island was urban by wilderness standards. For two hundred years the Ojibwe had summered on the mainland across the narrow channel, burning the rise behind their camp to cultivate blueberries. They planted fields of corn, potatoes, and other vegetables at the center of the island, and at the east end they buried their dead near sacred juniper rings. At "English Channel," just east of the island, was an eighteenth-century fur company post. Good whitewashed all the camp buildings and called the place White City. Flashing on the dark, distant shore, it was an easily visible landmark from the far southern side of Basswood Lake, even during a storm or by moonlight.[16]

Under Good's guidance, Swallow and Hopkins worked its way through the border lakes, culling the patchwork and swaths of ancient pine that had survived repeated forest fires. National lumber production was approaching peak levels—levels not achieved since. But while Good had mastered the challenges posed by geography, other factors created greater obstacles.[17]

On July 19, 1901, the citizens of Ely filed a complaint with Minnesota's attorney general against Swallow and Hopkins, alleging, first, that the more than ten million feet of logs stranded in Burntside Lake prevented recreation and, second, that as the company raised water levels to move these logs, "Irreparable damage is being done . . . the waters are washing out trees from the edges of islands." Good also had to reckon with inflating stumpage prices. As the pine stands thinned and competition increased, the average state auction price for a thousand board feet of pine stumpage rose from $1.81 in 1895 to $5.49 in 1900, reaching $8.30 by 1902. To make matters worse, competitors were drawing ever nearer to the border lakes.[18]

In mid-April 1900, officers from St. Croix Lumber—Minnesota's first lumber company, incorporated by pioneer Franklin Steele in 1838 at the Falls of St. Anthony—bought a mill site on Fall Lake from Robert Whiteside. Bert and Martin Torinus paid three hundred fifty thousand dollars for almost 100 million feet of standing pine in the Stony River country south of town. In August 1900, St. Croix Lumber Company decided against building a third mill and bought the Knox Lumber Company mill and its uncut lands instead. Knox withheld 11 million feet of sawn lumber and the planing mill from the deal, selling the lumber to Shepard, Morris and Company of Tonawanda, New York, and the planing mill to St. Croix the next year.[19]

The January 25, 1901, edition of the *Ely Miner* reported the total cuts of the three Winton companies for the previous year: St. Croix Lumber Company, 5 million board feet; Knox Lumber Company, 11 million board feet; and Fall Lake Lumber Company (the first and short-lived name of Swallow and Hopkins), 20 million board feet. Despite this early deficit, the St. Croix Lumber Company soon dominated the Winton/Ely scene. The oldest logging concern in the state, the company not only was well financed, well equipped, and well staffed, it also enjoyed dependable markets.

The Torinus brothers logged much of Whiteside's old claims east and south of Winton along the Kawishiwi and Stony Rivers and Birch and White Iron Lakes. Due to Whiteside's informed homesteading, they avoided railroad logging for many years, floating their cut to Fall Lake instead. The company bought more pinelands just northeast of Burntside, on the Low and Bass Lake chain; due north of Burntside, along North Arm Bay and up to Big Lake; and south to Trapper's Lake, high on the north slope of the Laurentian Divide, the headwaters of the Winton watershed. Contractors for the company were cutting from Lake Vermilion to Mud Creek and Burntside, including Simpson, McTiver, and Densmore, who continued to cut along the Duluth and Iron Range road from Tower, clearing the Johnson and Bear Island Lake area.[20]

By far the most challenging contract went to Tower pioneer E. S.

Howe, who agreed to begin a road twenty miles south along the Stony River, a stump- and rock-littered tract spanning some of the roughest country in the northland. A series of steep ridges and sheer rock faces forced the road to twist and turn into extraordinary contortions. Floating black spruce swamps and muskeg bog, impassable in the summer, lay between these cubist ridges. In winter the moist ground froze, heaving and fracturing roadbeds. Howe's crude road wound south from Ely, swinging across the Stony and Kawishiwi Rivers twenty-six miles to St. Croix's Headquarters Camp. From there it fell away south and east to McDougal Lake, where it turned and wound in with the Stony River, crossing the water when necessary, meandering south to the river's boggy beginnings high on the Laurentian Divide's north slope. By wagon it was a three-day trip from Ely to Camp Ten, located at Source Lake, the Roaring Stony River's origin. St. Croix spent over six thousand dollars per mile to build the famous Stony Tote Road, which was paved and renamed Highway 1 by St. Louis County in early fall 1921. It remains a tortured, winding, and buckled tract, a challenge to modern drivers even at speeds less than fifty miles per hour.[21]

St. Croix's Headquarters Camp, their version of Good's White City on Basswood, was twenty-six miles from Ely. Here the company warehoused and distributed supplies for its many camps along the Stony from more than a dozen log buildings that included storerooms, offices, barns, teamsters' quarters, a bunkhouse, a cook house and dining hall, a blacksmith shop, a carpenter shop, and a large wanigan or supply house. The area's stovepipe-sized trees were stood on end and chinked with oakum and moss to create these structures, the camp's appearance more like a zebra stockade than a white city.

Besides managing a geographical spread of timberlands larger than that of either Swallow and Hopkins or Knox, the Torinus brothers also had ambitious sawmill plans. They nearly doubled output in the old Knox mill by simply installing a two-sided band saw which allowed sawyers to cut on both strokes of the carriage. A new 700-light electric plant illuminated every corner of the operation so mills, offices, millpond, and yards could run twenty-four hours a day. A hulking hive-shaped brick burner powered St. Croix's bank of boilers, sending up plumes of black smoke from which sparks and glowing cinders zigzagged into the sky. The company built new boarding houses, company stores, and stables in Ely and developed a water- and steam-heat system for the residents of Winton. And they were always on the lookout for opportunities to innovate and increase production.[22]

As St. Croix's loggers cut farther and farther inland, they needed a replacement for their horses, which simply could not manage the weight of a sleigh full of logs in the steep Stony River country. From the Tower Lumber Company, the Torinus brothers bought a steam crawler, a machine that had proved effective in rugged Pike River country. A hybrid between a locomotive and a modern caterpillar tractor, the steam crawler was powered by a wood-fired boiler and a geared steam engine that drove cleated metal tracks. The sled directly behind the crawler held one man who stoked the furnace while above and in front of him another throttled the steam power. Away from the protection of the cab and the warmth of the boiler, a third man perched at the front above the runners, using a large wheel mounted between his knees to steer the long train. Locals never ceased to turn out when the crawlers thundered through Ely, the tracks clattering and throwing clots of frozen mud, ice, and snow, black smoke pouring from furnace stacks as they made their way to the Stony Road.[23]

A precursor to the bulldozer, the steam crawler represented the first awkward stirrings of industrial logging, a trend that would eventually allow a five-man crew using feller-bunchers, dozers, and trucks to do the work of a hundred jacks. Each crawler replaced about sixty jacks and thirty horses. In the Stony district the machines could drag twenty sleds, each loaded with ten to fifteen thousand board feet of logs, twenty miles in a day. Under the best of circumstances, a horse team could haul about thirty thousand board feet three miles. Steam crawlers were not perfect, however. Their cleated treads were fragile, often breaking in rough country, and the machines had no brakes or reverse gear, making them rather cumbersome. Still, they were the best solution to the rugged Stony territory, and St. Croix kept several in operation after 1906.[24]

Horses were still used for supplies. Leaving the main stables and offices in Ely, near the present-day lumberyard, Percherons pulled loaded wagons up the steep grade of Ely's Sheridan Street, their heads down and their broad shoulders heaving into the harnesses, for the three-day journey to the camp at Source Lake. Later, empty wagons rattled back into town, the horses' heads high and the teamsters riding the brakes, flatbeds filled with a thirsty gang of jacks instead of cargo. In these early years, the teams carried more than freight or passengers: they also carried news and verbal or written orders from the company office, delivered to and from the camps within days. But in 1906 the Torinus brothers began to string telephone lines through the woods, an innovation that increased efficiency even more than the steam crawlers had.[25]

Now jacks called the Ely warehouses directly when they needed equipment or replacement parts for the steam crawlers. The quarter-

A ST. CROIX LOG TRAIN
ix Lumber & Manufacturing Co.
Winton, Minnesota.

*Manned by a crew of four, a St. Croix steam crawler loaded with logs travels a winter road in the Stony River country around 1911.*

master shipped the needed parts out on the next wagon, saving many days in down time. Jacks could also coordinate the opening and closing of dams, thereby greatly reducing logjams. With telephones to spread the word when a jam began to form, jacks upriver could hold back the logs and prevent the situation from worsening. Finally, telephones became the most useful tool in fire suppression. Phones cut response time in half, provided accurate information as conditions changed, and allowed firefighters to coordinate plans and evacuations. Though some blazes still raged out of control, telephones helped save lives and were key to fire-fighting efforts.

These many innovations were expensive, and when natural forces on the border lakes turned against the Torinus brothers, they faltered. A drought in 1908 continued into 1909. Lack of snow seriously hindered logging operations and promised a dangerous fire season ahead. The summer was dry, but Superior National Forest rangers were able to suppress the few blazes that did begin. Despite another dry winter in 1909, Bert and Mart Torinus remained hopeful, purchasing on February 15, 1910, about 225 million board feet from the newly created Superior National Forest, the national forest's first recorded transaction. The "Birch Lake Sale" contained 100 million feet of white pine at seven dollars per thousand, 100 million feet of red pine (about 25 million of which had been killed in wildfires in 1908 and 1909) at six dollars per thousand, and 53 million feet comprised of spruce, tamarack, and jack pine at three dollars per thousand.[26]

Unfortunately for the Torinus brothers, the forests began to burn the moment the meager snow melted in 1910. The *Ely Miner* reported on April 15: "Fires Starting on Range. Region Dry and Danger is Grave." The St. Croix company was hit heavily early in the season, and when in mid-May Bert and Mart drove down the Stony Tote Road to check their losses after camps eighteen and twenty burned, they found the once wild river reduced to a muddy trickle, stranded logs beached on the riverbed, the air thick with smoke.[27]

Fires raged across the United States that entire summer. In just forty-eight hours, seventy-nine forest service firefighters burned to death in Idaho. Three billion acres in Washington, Montana, and Idaho were incinerated, sending smoke across the continent and darkening

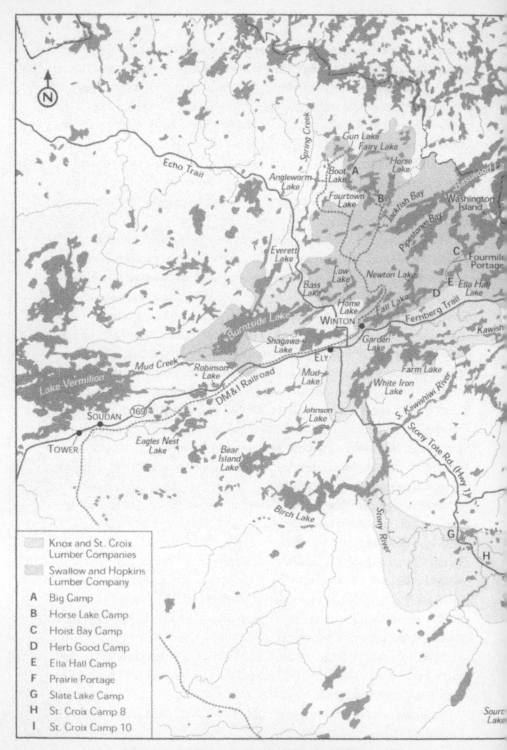

*Winton watershed (western half), showing select lumber camps*
*and lumber company holdings*

Knox and St. Croix
Lumber Companies

Swallow and Hopkins
Lumber Company

A  Big Camp
B  Horse Lake Camp
C  Hoist Bay Camp
D  Herb Good Camp
E  Ella Hall Camp
F  Prairie Portage
G  Slate Lake Camp
H  St. Croix Camp 8
I  St. Croix Camp 10

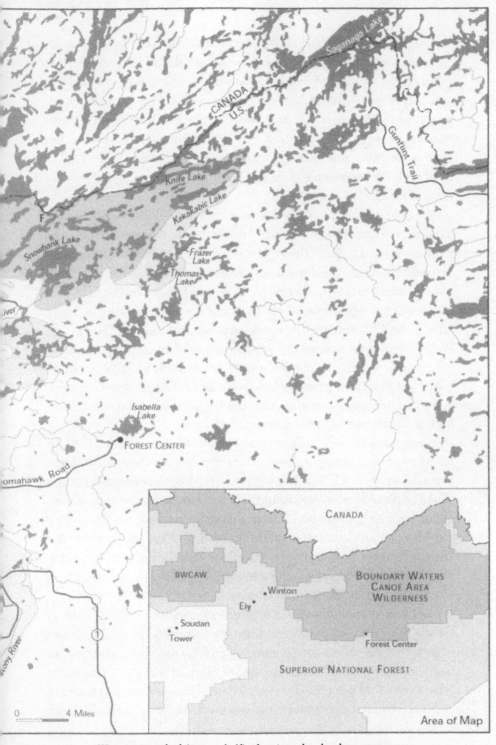

Sagamaga Lake

CANADA
U.S.

Gunflint Trail

Knife Lake

Kekakabic Lake

F

Snowbank Lake

Frazer
Lake

Thomas
Lake

...iver

Isabella
Lake

● FOREST CENTER

...omahawk Road

①

...ony River

CANADA

BWCAW

● Winton
Ely ●

● Soudan
Tower

BOUNDARY WATERS
CANOE AREA
WILDERNESS

● Forest Center

SUPERIOR NATIONAL FOREST

Area of Map

0            4 Miles

*Winton watershed (eastern half), showing select lumber camps
and lumber company holdings*

skies in New York. In April, fire blazed in Bayfield County, Wisconsin. By May huge fires began burning five hundred square miles of Minnesota forest, leveling Grand Marais on Lake Superior's north shore and threatening Duluth, Arnold, and Bemidji. Fire repeatedly approached the towns of Ely and Winton. The Birch Lake settlement burned, and still no rain came. As the fires subsided in November, the Torinus brothers, out of both money and luck, traveled to St. Paul to meet with timber baron F. E. Weyerhaeuser and Chicago lumberman Edward Hines.[28]

Just two years earlier, Weyerhaeuser and Hines had incorporated the Virginia and Rainy Lake Company in Virginia, Minnesota. The company claimed to operate the largest white-pine sawmill in the world, and it was voracious, pulling in logs from all corners of the northland. On November 21, 1910, Weyerhaeuser and Hines bought St. Croix Lumber Company's entire Winton operation, renaming it the St. Croix Lumber and Manufacturing Company. For $2.5 million, Hines and Weyerhaeuser now owned the Winton sawmill and planing mill, all of the company's residences, warehouses, and outbuildings, 300 million board feet of standing timber located in St. Louis and Lake Counties, and 50 million board feet of logs jammed in the rivers, stranded at landings, and scattered in random booms on lakes.[29]

Hines asked an associate from Hayward, Wisconsin, Thomas S. Whitten, to be general manager, offering him an option on twenty-five shares of capital stock worth fifty thousand dollars. Whitten moved to Ely and added a lath mill, picket mill, and box-board department that winter. One week after Swallow and Hopkins began its season's cut, the mill for the new St. Croix Lumber and Manufacturing Company opened. The Torinus brothers returned home to Stillwater, their departure marking the end of pioneer logging in the BWCAW. Weyerhaeuser, the Henry Ford of lumbering, stood poised to take over the northland.[30]

Similar to that of Robert Whiteside, Frederick Weyerhaeuser's biography is a great American immigrant success story. In an 1852 letter from Erie, Pennsylvania, to Niedersaulheim, Germany, an adventurous sister and her husband urged the rest of the family to join them in the New World. The Weyerhaeusers sold their farm, divided the proceeds, and placed shares in trust for those not yet twenty-one years old. Frederick, one of those minors, wrote: "We started about the middle of May and journeyed by boat down the Rhine to Rotterdam . . . got a boat to London . . . and took a sailing ship from London to New York. The voyage occupied about six weeks, and was somewhat rough at times, but I enjoyed every minute of it. . . . It was a great event."[31]

At twenty-one, his inheritance in hand, Frederick Weyerhaeuser went west. This time, a letter had come from another intrepid relative, as Weyerhaeuser recalled, "One of my father's cousins had gone to Edington, Illinois about 18 miles south of Rock Island, and her husband had bought a farm there. They sent us wonderful accounts of the richness of the prairie soil, and this stirred me up to go west." He arrived early in March and found work on a sawmill crew instead of toiling on the land. The mill's owner quickly promoted the bright young man, and by 1857 Weyerhaeuser controlled his first lumberyard. His method to achieve success—so simple, so common—"lay simply in my readiness to work. I never counted the hours, or stopped until I had finished what I had in hand."[32]

In those days there was intense competition among the many Mississippi River sawmills, each jockeying for logs from upriver and for markets on the Great Plains. The river's periodic floods and droughts contributed uncertainty, so Weyerhaeuser traveled north to see the operations there—the forests, the transportation routes, the potential—searching to gain control of his supply. He later wrote: "When I first saw the fine timber on the Chippewa, I wanted to say nothing about it. It was like the feeling of a man who has discovered a hidden treasure. If only Weyerhaeuser and Denkman could control this they would have an almost inexhaustible supply of the very best timber in the world."[33]

Five miles below Wabasha, Minnesota, on the Wisconsin side of the Mississippi, a meandering branch of the Chippewa River leaves the main stream at Round Hill and joins the Mississippi alongside the larger Chippewa River just above the town of Alma, Wisconsin. The confluence of these three forms a backwater eddy where currents slow and gravel settles into a gentle bar.[34]

At this sandbar lumbermen built the largest logging boom ever constructed. They used the naturally slower waters to gather logs from the many watersheds upstream, sorting them by the various stamp marks set into the end of each log the winter before, separating each firm's logs from those cut by other firms on the watershed. At Beef Slough booming works, buyers came to place orders for their mills. Between twelve and fifteen hundred men built rafts for the companies downstream, each raft composed of two halves made of three brails—a log raft six hundred feet long and forty-five feet wide. The jacks used the largest white pine, the so-called cork pine, to build the sides of these brails, flattening the ends of the pine, boring a two-inch hole nine inches deep, and fastening a heavy three-link chain with a wide-headed oak or ironwood plug to hold the chain in place. These floating corrals had just enough flexibility to travel the meandering Mississippi.[35]

*It took plenty of workers and a good deal of organization to divide up various companies' logs and float them into booms to send downriver. This site on the Mississippi's West Newton Slough was photographed circa 1890.*

Once a boom was ready, the men floated all the company's logs into it to fill the order, binding the rafts with half-inch crosswires to preserve their shape. When all the booms were coupled together they made a raft 275 feet wide and 600 feet long containing 800,000 to one million feet of logs and weighing 3,500 tons. The largest raft ever built, 270 feet wide and 1,450 feet long, contained nine million board feet of logs.[36]

For many years the critical market for the national timber industry, Beef Slough saw more than 11 billion board feet of logs float through its boom between 1867 and 1905. Containing one-fifth of the nation's pre-settlement supply of timber, the Mississippi River watershed, including the Chippewa, Black, Wisconsin, and St. Croix Rivers, sent nearly 47 billion board feet of logs downstream between 1837 and 1915, when the last raft, towed by the *Ottumwa Belle,* left Hudson, Wisconsin, bound for Fort Madison, Iowa.[37]

Competition among Wisconsin lumbering firms for this prodigious supply was fierce and sometimes violent, costing millions in lost efficiency. But when a flood destroyed the boom in 1870 and struggling companies teetered on the brink of ruin, Weyerhaeuser seized the opportunity to gain the upper hand. On November 1, 1870, he and two other Mississippi sawmill operators, Mr. Schricker and Elijah Swift, leased the wrecked boom for five years. These three, under Weyerhaeuser's leadership, propositioned other lumber firms along the river to join them in an effort to take over the rich Chippewa Valley. On December 28 and 29, seventeen firms formed a new corporation, the Mississippi River Logging Company, and bought controlling interest in the Beef Slough Boom Company. As compensation each owner was guaranteed about six million board feet of logs annually. Weyerhaeuser's new company charged seventy-five cents per thousand feet for logs and two cents per thousand feet of crossties sorted and boomed for any given company. As Weyerhaeuser's warm personality eased tensions, the disparate, distrustful interests, many of which had ruthlessly vied against each other for years, joined under his leadership. With better organization and decreased competition, in 1872 Beef Slough had its record year.[38]

Weyerhaeuser now controlled a critical aspect of both his market and the transportation system; next he needed to guarantee supply.

Without supply there was no stability, no way to justify the enormous capital investment required of an industrial wood products enterprise. It was difficult, in the early days, to obtain a massive block of pineland and assure a steady timber supply years before need, for lumbermen could not own or hold land until it was part of the public domain. And, once the land was public, the auction system, the homestead law, and other avenues of private land acquisition favored small lots owned by independent farmers—a reflection of the founding fathers' desire to foster a landed, agrarian democracy. Of course, this system had huge loopholes through which stepped many frontier land speculators—Whiteside on the Winton watershed being just one example.

However, around the time of the Civil War, in a radical philosophical shift, the federal government began offering huge swaths of the public domain to encourage the development of transportation and education. In the decades following the war, the railroads received 200 million acres in land grants, one-eighth of the country. Twenty-two percent of the territory that became Montana went to railroad barons, the most famous of whom was James J. Hill, Weyerhaeuser's neighbor in St. Paul, Minnesota. Hill eventually sold millions of acres of heavily timbered Pacific Northwest lands to Weyerhaeuser, for just dollars an acre. Congress made title to these lands transferable, and so, to defray the costs of building railroads, wagon roads, and canals, railroad barons sold land they did not need as right of way. Then, in 1862 Congress passed the Morrill Act, giving each state thirty thousand acres of non-mineral land for each of its congressional representatives, intending that the money raised from land sales would support state universities.[39]

In the 1860s, university founder Ezra Cornell acquired almost five hundred thousand acres of prime pine stands in the Chippewa River Valley under the Morrill Act. The Cornell grant was especially fortuitous for Weyerhaeuser's new Mississippi River Logging Company: on October 26, 1875, Weyerhaeuser bought fifty thousand acres of Cornell's land for ten dollars an acre at seven percent interest over a ten-year span.[40]

Both Weyerhaeuser and Whiteside understood that the value of virgin pine stumpage, unlike that of finished lumber, increases steadily. A large supply of uncut timber justified the expense of huge milling facilities, extensive logging railroads, and nationwide distribution outlets, a modern wood products industry. Weyerhaeuser turned his attentions north, taking over smaller operators who could no longer compete, claiming smaller trees, remote stands, second growth, cutting everything pioneer loggers like Swallow and Hopkins and the Torinus brothers had not. Technological advances had made previously unmarketable timber valuable, and Weyerhaeuser cut and milled these so-called pulp trees.

Originally there was only one type of logging, the saw log harvest. A saw log, usually twelve or more inches in diameter, is suitable for making dimension lumber. During the cut of Minnesota's forests, the size of trees deemed harvestable steadily decreased. At first the trees were so large that, on average, four and a half logs scaled at a thousand board feet. By 1904, the size of the trees being cut had diminished until an average of thirteen logs were required to scale a thousand board feet. Not until the end of the harvest, when saw logs were becoming scarce, did lumber companies begin to cut pulp logs, small trees with a shorter growing cycle of twenty to seventy years. Harvested not for their potential as dimension lumber but for their wood fiber, pulp logs are shredded and then reorganized into a variety of products including paper, strand board, and laminated beams. Originally the favored pulp species were hemlock and spruce, but as even these supplies were exhausted the industry switched to balsam and aspen. As a reflection of the evolution from saw logs to pulp logs, the USFS now measures timber harvest in square feet of wood fiber, not in board feet.[41]

In the old days, no logger would cut aspen or live in a camp built with poplar. Some claimed that Canadian

*Timber baron Frederick Weyerhaeuser brought industrialized logging to Minnesota's north woods.*

camps used poplar to make coffins, others that Christ's cross was poplar, and therefore the tree was bad luck. The prejudice against aspen had less to do with superstition and more to do with the wood's inferiority. Having none of the qualities of pine, aspen mars easily, rots quickly, is not particularly strong, and does not float well. But aspen is prodigious, growing either from seed or sucker, thriving in disturbed, cutover areas, invading cleared pine forest with as many as forty thousand stems per acre the spring following logging. Today, aspen is the predominate species and makes up the bulk of timber cut from Superior National Forest.[42]

As the big mills in Minneapolis and Stillwater had more and more trouble finding dimension-quality trees, Weyerhaeuser converted his operations to the production of paper, laminates, and chip board. The *Ely Miner* wrote:

> The paper mill follows the lumberman, and is sure indication of the passing of the pine forest. The third mill (paper) for northern Minnesota has just been opened for business at Grand Rapids, with an investment of over $300,000, and the headwaters of the Mississippi now turn the wheels of commerce, making the fairy tales of a generation ago stale, flat and unprofitable compared with the reality of today.[43]

In 1917, George Long, a Wisconsin lumberman who had gone west early to manage Weyerhaeuser's newly purchased Pacific Northwest lands, wrote to a friend who had stayed in Wisconsin:

> I suppose you never expected to live long enough to see the day when the hemlock stumpage around Hurley and Gile would yield a better price . . . than did the old Montreal River Lumber Company's cork pine which we labored with in the gloomy years of 1893 to 1900. . . . One thing is quite manifest to my mind, that the men who stayed in Wisconsin and cleaned up all the different kinds of wood that were left, after the white pine was cleaned out, did not make a very bad guess, and in many instances they have done better than the ambitious chap who went out where timber was in bunches and cheap and good.[44]

In spring 1899, Weyerhaeuser opened a pulp mill in Cloquet, Minnesota, the largest and fastest of its kind worldwide. Then, in 1902 DuPont developed a process using wood pulp to make both good-quality paper and rayon, the first synthetic fiber, giving Weyerhaeuser a huge market for his new products. By then Weyerhaeuser owned part of eighteen mills in three states plus the Minnesota River Logging Company and the Beef Slough Manufacturing, Booming, Log Driving, and Transportation Company, and he held stock and sat on the boards of most of Wisconsin and Minnesota's lumbering firms. Eventually he took control of the lands and mills of the St. Croix, Swallow and Hopkins, Knox, Hines, Potlatch, Northern, and Pine Tree lumber companies. The power of Weyerhaeuser's integrated corporate structure coupled with the expense of new technologies forced out family operators like Knox, Whiteside, and the Torinus brothers and other small-time outfits.[45]

Weyerhaeuser had almost exclusive control of logging operations on the Chippewa, St. Croix, and Upper Mississippi Rivers, an area containing some of the richest pineries left in the world. He owned timberland, mills, transportation networks, and retail outlets, making the Weyerhaeuser companies the most economically integrated organization in the Upper Midwest and allowing him to set the price for lumber from the Great Lakes to the Rocky Mountains. By 1913 his companies owned 95 billion board feet of stumpage, 4.3 percent of the privately held standing timber in the United States. In Minnesota, just six companies owned nearly 54 percent of the pine stands.[46]

Despite Weyerhaeuser's conquest of the Torinus brothers' operation, for a short time Swallow and Hopkins was able to continue its harvest of remote virgin pine stands to the north. Although in 1911 Swallow and Hopkins sold Fourmile Portage, Prairie Portage, dams, sluiceways, and other facilities to Weyerhaeuser and Edward Hines for nineteen thousand dollars, two years earlier the company had built a railroad to Jackfish Bay and Angleworm Lake, and a later extension—connecting this route with the mill via the Duluth and Iron Range road at Winton—allowed it to operate there for a time, though on a limited scale.[47]

After selling the Fourmile, Swallow and Hopkins worked north of Fall Lake and west of Basswood. While all the logging companies in the area had long cut timber near Burntside Lake, the land just to the north and east, the area that had originally given the lake its name, had grown up in jack pine. Too small to bother with when the white pine cut began, these stands were still relatively untouched in 1910. While Swallow and Hopkins originally cut only white and red pine, by the time it acquired this land it was selling pulp—jack pine, aspen, fir, and spruce—to the Cloquet pulp mill. The company paid Weyerhaeuser freight charges to use Good's old Fourmile Portage as it cut remnant pine in the distant corners of its original land holdings. The cleared, mostly burnt timberland left behind was released as tax forfeiture.[48]

*A forest of Norway pine dwarfs a horse-drawn wagon and its passengers near Elbow Lake.*

Meanwhile, Weyerhaeuser was reaching deeper into the heart of what would become the BWCAW. Minnesota State Auditor stumpage records show that in 1911 and 1912 the St. Croix Lumber and Manufacturing Company bought about 432 million feet of standing pine. In the next years it logged east past Knife Lake, cleared out the Kekakabic-Frazer-Thomas Lakes area, built a winter tote road from Ensign Lake to Lunar Lake, and opened up Saganaga Lake to logging. The company estimated that with the new mill cutting forty thousand board feet per day, it had enough timber to run for ten years—about 146 million board feet. After Swallow and Hopkins sold its mill and logging railroad to Weyerhaeuser in 1922, he continued to harvest second growth—jack pine, spruce, and poplar in the cutovers—as well as stands of virgin pulpwood in the lakes region, delivering the logs directly to the paper mills in Cloquet and bypassing Winton completely.[49]

By 1920 transporting logs was no longer expensive, and horses, steam crawlers, and even railroads were nearly obsolete. As early as 1914 St. Croix Lumber and Manufacturing had begun using trucks in the woods. In summer 1914, when the company had about sixty horses engaged solely to transport goods down the Stony Tote Road, a group of experts from Chicago visited Ely to run preliminary tests on the road. After a few trials ended in failure, one truck in September failing to "fill the bill" and another in October lacking the power to climb the road's steep hills, St. Croix ordered a larger truck, a Jeffrey forty-horsepower, four-wheel drive vehicle. In November the *Ely Miner* ran the following story:

> The St. Croix company it seems has at last solved the matter of toting supplies to the Stony River country quite satisfactorily. The new four-wheel drive truck is making a regular trip each day to headquarters with a two ton load. The truck leaves at about 8:30 in the morning and returns 3:30 in the afternoon. At the rate it travels, three trips in two days can easily be made. The truck is also capable of hauling a trailer with a two-ton load. The same trip heretofore has required the services of six horses and a teamster for two days. In all probability more trucks will be put on later. The roads to headquarters are at present in excellent condition.

Easier to operate, requiring fewer men, cheaper to buy and maintain, able to reach remote areas to haul even small stands of trees economically, trucks were perfect for the ragged patchwork of forest left after forty years of lumbering.[50]

By 1913, just three years after Weyerhaeuser took control of the company, St. Croix Lumber and Manufacturing began releasing its cleared land to the old St. Croix Lumber Company, now just a shell corporation. Eventually venerable St. Croix Lumber, the state's first lumber company, lost these desolate assets for back taxes and folded; the land, devoid of trees, burnt and barren, returned to the state as tax forfeiture property.

Robert Whiteside and his brothers had claimed the pine on the Winton watershed in the 1880s. Sam Knox and his grandson-in-law, Billy Winton, had begun the cut in 1891. Swallow and Hopkins, Herb Good, and the Torinus brothers had installed the infrastructure. But it was Frederick Weyerhaeuser who finished clearing the land. Weyerhaeuser brought the full power of industrial technology and the integrated corporation to bear on what would become the BWCAW, marking the beginning of the third phase of human management of the border lakes. Beginning in 1910 he industrialized the north woods, reached into the most remote corners, and snatched up and sold any remaining isolated pines as well as vast areas of other virgin forest types like jack pine, black spruce, balsam, and aspen. In the process, he emerged as the most powerful timber man in the world, personally controlling an area larger than many countries.

# 4

## Lumberjack Life

*I had a job in the great north woods,*
*working as a cook for a spell.*
*But I never did like it all that much*
*and one day the ax just fell.*

BOB DYLAN, "Tangled Up in Blue"

---

A PRODUCT OF THE AMERICAN FRONTIER, boomtowns rose with the raucous, rowdy, and lawless splendor of new settlements beyond the ken of civilization. Blooming suddenly and with great flourish, they disappeared just as quickly, collapsing beneath the weighty veneer of civilization as the frontier became settled. Winton was one of the last Minnesota boomtowns to prosper and then atrophy.

In 1893, the year Knox Mill opened, Winton had a population of one hundred and boasted one company store, one stable, one boarding house, and twenty-four frame houses. The next year a teacher arrived and the company built a school for the town's eighteen children. By 1900 Winton's population was six hundred. The following year the Swallow and Hopkins company alone employed 450 mill hands. By 1911, twelve hundred lumberjacks worked in the woods and two thousand people lived in Winton.

The sweet, resinous smell of freshly sawn lumber permeated Winton, not to mention copious dust from the mills, a torment to Winton's housekeepers. The high-pitched, metallic scream of the saws provided a constant backdrop, the shrill metronome of the sawmill whistle the town's heartbeat, signaling shift changes, weddings, funerals, rounds in a boxing match, even baseball victories. In winter, with the jacks out in the woods and the sawmill supplied only by rail, the pulse was slow. In spring, however, as the jacks rode logs downriver into town, the pulse quickened considerably.

After the long, dark, cold winters, spring came suddenly. With the ice out of the lakes and rivers, the jacks were ready to "burn out the grease." Townsfolk kept children indoors and respectable women avoided the "business districts," where raucous laughter boomed out of saloon and bagnio windows. Woods workers crowded the boardwalks as bunkos solicited them from saloon doorways or bordello balconies. The prone forms of lumberjacks sleeping off benders littered haylofts, horse stalls, alleys, sheds, and even the foul, muddy gutters.

After nine months in a logging camp, a lumberjack's thirst for women and drink was nearly unquenchable. Logging was hard work, dangerous and demanding. But the rules established to maintain control of hundreds of men living in close quarters were perhaps more tormenting than the labor. Life in camp was so restricted that the jacks tended to overcompensate when they first got to town in the spring.

No skirts or smilo, that is, women, were allowed in camp: maternal or medicinal, it made no difference. The companies forbid thermometers so jacks could not complain that it was too cold to work. New recruits quickly learned never to sit on another man's bunk or on the deacon seat in front of it, never to change bunks or touch another man's clothing, tobacco, "stags," or slippers. Lumber camps were like loose confederations of fiefdoms, and as the jacks passed from one realm to the next they had to serve different masters and abide different rules. In the bunkhouse, the bull cook's domain, jacks could talk only in low tones. The bull cook regulated the heat, too, and jacks were forbidden to adjust the skylights and stoves.

Similarly, cookees ruled the mess halls, which were usually finer structures, and warmer, than the bunkhouses. Without electricity, gas, or plumbing the cooks fed hundreds of hungry and demanding men every day. Since nothing shut down an operation faster than food poisoning, the cook's rules were strict, carrying harsh penalties if broken.

The one person in camp a jack could absolutely not afford to offend was the cook, and new men quickly learned the established routine. Platters of food steamed on the tables as the jacks filed into the cookhouse. Without a word, everyone went directly to his assigned seat at rough-hewn benches worn smooth and dark and shiny by canvas duck and wool stag pants. New men or guests hung by the door until a cookee set a place at the foot of one of the plank-topped, oilcloth-covered tables.

Huge wood-burning stoves separated the kitchen from the dining hall. Screened buildings abounded with hams, bacon, and grouse, fish, deer, or moose supplied by the Ojibwe or skid row spikers—retired lumberjacks who lived in shanties along the skid trails. Another small building served as pantry and held flour, cornmeal, dried fruit, clear corn syrup, pickled meats, and a barrel or two of oysters for Christmas dinner. Firewood was stored in the dingle or alleyway, a roofed space between the kitchen and the bunkhouse. The cook and cookees slept in bunks at the back of the kitchen.

There was no conversation in a dining hall: no announcements from the foreman, not even a word from the cook. Jacks whispered and pointed to tin platters when they wanted more sow belly (pickled salt pork), dried pea soup, fresh bread, oleo margarine, beans, or raisin pie. All the dishes and utensils being tin, the forks, serving spoons, and knives raised a cheap cacophony that would have drowned out any conversation. The plates, though boiled sterile and usually bitter with bleach, were so greasy from lack of scrubbing that the jacks claimed they could write their names on them with a finger.

The food, however, was tasty and abundant. Servings were unlimited, for there was almost no limit to the amount a man who had worked hard for twelve hours in subzero temperatures could eat. Jacks demanded good grub, and many would leave camps for others that had better cooks, sometimes choosing a good cook over a good foreman, following him from company to company. In some camps, the cooks earned as much as $2.50 a day, two and one-half times more than the lumberjacks.

After dinner the jacks gathered in the bunkhouse, the teamsters at one end playing four-way cribbage, the sawyers at a deacon's bench telling stories, darning socks, or patching their rubbers. The jacks smoked pipes, not cigarettes. Some foremen wouldn't hire a jack who smoked "pimp sticks." Just inside the door a leaded basin served as washstand, two towels available for the roomful of men. A wood stove glowed at the center of the room, the jacks' wool clothing and socks drying on a rack above it or hung from nails set into the roof beams. Two tiers of double, straw-filled bunks lined the walls end-to-end like miniature stalls in a crowded two-story livery. But while each horse in a livery got its own stall, in a lumber camp the men slept two to a bunk. The deacon seat doubled as a step to the top bunks. Daylight cascaded in from numerous chinks between the log walls, and beams of light stabbed into the room from holes in the roof.

In the bunkhouse the older men held forth, telling stories about the cuts in Maine and Michigan and Wisconsin. They argued about the

*Lumberjacks momentarily suspend their bunkhouse storytelling around a coal-burning stove.*

heaviest load ever hauled, the largest whore, the swiftest river, the size of the largest white pine tree in all of Minnesota, a tree so big it took three days to walk around it. Winton camps had their own lore, about the time the switchman at Hopkins Junction got drunk, forgot to throw the switch, and sent a fully loaded train of logs barreling out onto the dead-end trestle on Fall Lake, sparks flying from the impotent brakes, the engineer and crew leaping to safety as the train thundered off the end and crashed into the lake, the hot engine sending up billows of steam when it hit the water. And local teamsters often told about a cross-lake haul late one spring, when the ice stretched under the weight of the loaded sleigh so that it seemed to sit in a shallow bowl. The teamster heard the ice moan and then the rifle-crack as it broke, and he, the loaded sled, and his six-horse team plunged into the icy waters of Burntside Lake. The horses—the teamster's livelihood—quickly became tangled in their traces, and when the man tried to cut them loose the panicked animals thrashed him to death with their hooves. Unable to regain the ice, they drowned, and their bloated bodies floated the lake that summer until the Ely town council declared them a health hazard and forced the company to remove them.

Usually around nine o'clock the men went to their bunks. The bull cook turned the kerosene lights low, stoked the fire, and left. The men crunched and crackled on their straw pallets, scratching at the blue jackets, crumbs, gray backs, or seam squirrels that infested every camp. The fire burned hotter, and the stove metal creaked and popped as it expanded. After the room settled down, the sound of snoring rumbled in the dark. Then, just before daylight, the bull cook, often a jack too old to work in the woods but with no other place to go, came in and roused the teamsters. The teamsters rose first to go to the barns and feed, water, and harness the horses for the day. The bull cook put more wood into the fire, and shortly after he left, at perhaps five o'clock, the road crew came in from the ice roads.

In 1888, before logging was under way in the border lakes, a director of the State Forestry Commission of Michigan claimed it cost a thousand dollars per mile to prepare a roadbed for a snowplow and sprinkling cart. The ice roads built in northern Minnesota almost certainly cost more. A marvel, these roads testified to the simple, elegant utility and strength of frozen water. The roadmen worked at night, when there was no traffic, when it was colder and the roads froze fast and hard. During summer jacks grubbed out the next year's ice road, felled big trees, and leveled stumps to clear a right of way. They blasted or pried rocks to level a grade, for horses could not haul up steep inclines. They lined up ten-foot logs across the roadway and made a floating corduroy bridge across swamps. At the first snow the

*Maintaining winter roads for the lumber camps was a full-time job. Men from Alger Smith and Company's camp eight, Cook County, break out a road in preparation for the sprinkler sled, circa 1916.*

cutters went out to pack the roads, their heavy sleds making ruts for the sprinkler.[1]

The sprinkler was an eight-by-twelve-by-four-foot-high water tank mounted on heavy sleigh runners. A full tank weighed about five tons. The sprinkler was built with a tongue on both ends because it was often easier to move the six-horse teams than to turn the sled. Out on the lakes, crews lowered barrels into holes cut in the ice and used a horse to cross-haul the filled barrel up two parallel poles to the top of the tank. A wood stove set into the water, the tank caulked tightly around the fire door, kept the water hot, and kerosene or fuel oil lamps kept the sprinklers from freezing when temperatures dipped far below zero. When the jacks reached the place in the road they wanted to ice, they pulled corks from the bungholes at the tank's corners and the sprinklers wet the snow. They watered the roads over and over again, building up ice many inches thick.[2]

When the ice was laid, the road crew brought out the groover, two massive timbered sleigh runners with steel blades mounted like a carpenter's plane on the bottom. Six-horse teams pulled the groover, shaving inverse rails to hold the runners of the logging sleds and help keep the heavy sleds on the narrow roads. Logging sleds had runners five inches thick, eleven inches high, and nine feet long, set seven feet and four inches apart. An empty sled weighed five tons, but when loaded with pine logs it could weigh as much as one hundred and fifty tons. The crews built up the ice through the coldest part of the winter and groomed it in warmer spring weather. The ice roads often lasted long after the lakes had thawed and the woods were free of snow. The lumberjack description of border lakes weather, "Nine months of good sledding and three of bad," was not all hyperbole.[3]

When the road crew returned from their night's work, the funky sourness of sweat-soaked wool filled the bunkhouse as they removed their pacs and mackinaws, hanging them near the stove to dry. Pacs, or rubbers, were waterproof to a degree, but more than that they were warm and comfortable. The ribbed rubber soles gave a jack some traction on the ice roads and in deep snow. The thick wool felt liners kept his feet warm in temperatures far below zero, even when he had to stand at a landing or sit on a sleigh all day. Local cobblers made variations on these shoes, and drummers traveled the woods supplying the many camps.

Another specialized shoe, caulked logger's boots were made for walking in the woods and on logs. The caulks, steel spikes set in rows across the sole, bit into even wet, barkless logs. The top of the boot was like any other, heavy leather treated with neat's-foot or mink oil, a one-piece tongue to keep a jack's feet dry, and laces that tied above the ankle for support. The business end was the sole, with its high instep and heel that fit the curve of a log the way a cowboy boot fits a stirrup. On level ground the heel threw a man slightly forward, giving him the sensation of walking downhill.

As the road crew climbed into their bunks, the other men rose and dressed in the dark. They might talk about that day's labors—a sawyer's strategy for felling a particular tree perhaps—discuss a new saw set, or consider the various attributes of different shapes and weights of axes. The teamsters had usually returned from feeding and harnessing the horses by the time the cookee blew a ragged reveille on his tin gut-horn. Breakfast was hot cakes, corn syrup, oleo margarine, beans, and fatback. The jacks ate quickly, tin spoons moving from mouth to plate to mouth in an accelerated rhythm broken only to wash down sticky beans with a swallow of scalding-hot chicory coffee.

As the sun rose they walked out to "the show," passing the "road monkeys" or "Blue Jays," who were busy preparing the roads for the day's traffic. The monkeys armed themselves with only a broom, a scoop shovel, and an ax, but their humble tools did not properly reflect the importance of their position. Their work began where the ice road left the barns and continued to the end of the line, as they scooped manure from the ice before the dark dung could absorb sunlight, melt into the ice, and break up the road. They cleared any downed trees or limbs, and in places where the road was worn thin they shoveled snow into the tracks and tamped it in place. On the steep downhill grades they littered straw in the ruts to slow the sleighs so they would not overtake the horses or break loose from the ruts and tip, burying both driver and horses beneath tons of logs. This was a studied skill, for too much straw would stop a heavy sleigh, always difficult to get moving again, and if the sled stopped too suddenly, the logs would be thrown forward onto the driver and horses. On short, very steep sections the road monkeys used a barienger brake, which controlled a drum wound with heavy cable that lowered loaded logging sleds down particularly steep or difficult grades. On a logging show the "hay hill road monkey's" manure scoop was a scepter, not a stable boy's burden.[4]

Work at the choppings was also well orchestrated and refined. The white pine in northern Minnesota often grew to a height of two hundred feet, with trunk sizes as great as six feet in diameter. Temperatures sometimes plunged to sixty degrees below zero, the snow standing three feet deep and often deeper. At the day's work area, the axe man, called a notcher or undercutter, waded through the snow to chip-in-a-zee with his two-bit ax. A good undercutter was so accurate that he could drive a six-foot pole into the earth by dropping a tree on it, what jacks called "driving Paul Bunyan's tent stake."

After the undercutter, a sawing crew set to work from the back side, the notcher directing the saw placement and angle. As the cut progressed, the sawyers drove wedges into the kerf to keep the weight of the tree from pinching the saw and sprinkled kerosene to dissolve sap on the saw blade and keep it running smoothly. The sawyers worked in a beautiful rhythm. The tone of a crosscut's song changed as the blade sank deeper into the heart of the tree, ringing a different note as each man pulled. Greenhorns turned the chore into a hackneyed staccato of grunts and hacks and swearing, the saw buckling on the backstroke, the rhythm off and broken. But two experienced sawyers were pure power, conservation of effort and poetry of motion. As the sawyers sweated, their mustaches, beards, and eyebrows became ice-coated and their soaked wool shirts crackled like cellophane. When the saw breached, the tree leaned, gained momentum, and fell from the sky. The sawyers called out, "Timberrrr!" and quickly walked away from the trunk. That was the moment. When the tree came down it was a moment frozen in time.

Save for the felling of the tree, logging was nothing more than dirty, dangerous, and poorly paid work, taking a man's best years and leaving him broken and poor. Yet the logger is a romanticized figure. Unlike other trades, a lumberjack's hard-packed life has blossomed into myth, the most famous being Paul Bunyan and his blue ox, Babe. Hank Stamper, Ken Kesey's larger-than-life portrait of a Pacific Northwest logger, stomps across the pages of American letters, the most hardy of rugged pioneer individualists. Loggers represent like few other professions the never-ending metaphorical man-against-nature grudge match that dominates so much of American fiction. Some things mesmerize all: a view from a high outlook, waves pounding on a beach, the curved expanse of horizon spread out behind. When the call of "Tree!" or "Timber!" rings out on a job, all heads turn. Even men without a standing tree or limb anywhere near pause from their work to watch the big trees fall. When one of those giants swept out of the sky where it had stood for so long, the mundane mixed with the mythical.

The swampers scrambled atop the fallen trees and walked the trunks, stripping away branches with an ax and marking the tree every eighteen and one-half feet, standard log length, for the sawyers. Sometimes they bucked away the bark so the log was easier to skid. After the sawyers cut it to length, the swampers rolled the logs over with cant hooks and axed the rest of the branches. The swampers, typically immigrants and lads, also cleared brush and undergrowth from the chopping so the jacks had a clean place to drop their trees and enough room to swing an ax or wield a saw. Swampers cut skid trails on which the teamsters could drag logs from the woods to a landing beside the ice road.

Like the bull cook and the cookee, the woods boss had his own set of dictums, but these usually required little enforcement. Cutting down these behemoths was dangerous work. Men who flaunted the rules risked not only their own lives but those of the men working near them. These many rules were all grounded in matters of safety:

Never carry an ax over your shoulder, file the blade, knock limbs from frozen timber with the backside, or use it to pound a wedge. Never use another man's cant hook, ax, saw, or other tool without permission. Never begin chopping or sawing into a tree before checking for any dead limbs that might fall—these were known as "widow makers." Always holler "Timber," and walk away from the trunk at a forty-five-degree angle as the tree falls. If a tree snags on another tree, never try to knock it down by felling another tree on top of it or felling the tree supporting it. Instead, get a team of horses and pull it free.

When maneuvering a log in the brush, have the horses swing it into position and then pull it straight out to the skid trail. Never let the horses pull while swinging a log: they might stumble and cut themselves with their spiked shoes. On a cold day stop often so the horses can catch their wind. Never sit down to lunch until the horses are blanketed, watered, and fed. Never criticize or sass the top loader or boss. Yell "Timber!" when felling a tree, "Break!" when breaking a skid way, and "Trip!" when unloading sleighs or rail cars, and yell loudly enough so that everyone on the crew can hear. When parking a loaded sled, stop and start several times for short distances to cool the runners so they won't freeze into the ice.[5]

After the swampers and sawyers had finished their tasks, the teamsters used a single horse, a chain, and skidding tongs called "dogs" or "timber tongs" to drag the log lengths from the chopping to the landing. When there wasn't much snow, they rolled the butt end of the logs onto small drays or sleds known as "go-devils" and slid them to the ice road. Jacks at the landing used poles and chains and sweat to roll the logs into stacks. When a full load was laid out, a teamster came by with a sled, and the top loader stacked the logs onto the timbered crib.[6]

Top loading was the most dangerous job in the camp. The top loader propped two long poles against the side of the sled angling down to the log. He wrapped a loading line around the middle of the log, ran the free end over the sled through a jammer—a huge cranelike tripod and pulley rig—and down to a team of horses. As the horses pulled, the log rolled up the poles and onto the sled, the top loader positioning it with a cant hook. In the early days, before the sleds had side stakes, the load had to be balanced and held by corner bind chains, wrapped at the corners and over the top of the load. It took some time to fill a sled, the load often rising to over sixteen feet in height. As the top loaders added more and more weight, the sleighs settled into the ruts of the ice road; oftentimes the pressure generated enough heat to melt the ice and freeze the runners fast. Once the sleigh was full the loaders whacked the runners with large wooden mauls, the Percherons pulled gee, then haw, and slowly the cumbersome mass began to move. The horses toiled deliberately, their hooves driving up and down like pistons, their spiked shoes churning crushed ice, the teamster behind them clucking and slapping the reins. The heavy sleigh timbers and stiff harnesses creaked and snapped with the weight. The runners hissed along the hoary ruts. Slowly the horses built momentum, then plodded along the ice road, sometimes as far as eight miles, to the banking grounds on the nearest waterway.

All winter the jacks felled trees, bucked them to length, loaded them onto sleds, hauled them out of the woods, and banked them on the frozen lakes or rivers. Some banking areas were huge, with many millions of board feet waiting for ice out. Here state scalers and clerks from the various local companies recorded board-foot measures and stamped each log end with the owner's registered mark. Clerks wrote the board-

*An axe man for the Alger-Smith Lumber Company observes*
*as two jacks work a crosscut saw through a felled pine.*

foot measure on the ends of the logs with a heavy grease pencil attached to the end of a scaling stick and tallied the totals in a record book for the company and the state. Some of the sawyer crews and teamsters were paid for each cut made or log hauled; the jacks' estimates always seemed to be higher than the company's. The jacks called the rulers "cheat sticks," "moneymakers," "robber's canes," and "swindle sticks," labeling those that wielded them simply "cheaters."

In the spring, life revolved around "the drive." As the daylight-to-dark workday of the lumberjack became longer, there was an increased urgency to move the logs before the ice roads melted. When the eerie sound of the lake and river ice groaning and fracturing in loud, echoing booms was heard in the camps, the jacks knew that any logs left in the woods were stranded until next winter, by which time they might well be lost in a fire or destroyed by boring insects. As the sun's daily path rose higher, more men went from cutting to hauling, from the woods to the rivers and lakes, from the skid trails to the railroad tracks.

The blacksmith, who had spent his winter re-shoeing horses that had thrown their spikes and building the huge water tanks, groove cutters, and log hauling sleds, spent his springs building wanigans and bateaus. A wanigan, in addition to being the company store, was also the name of a floating camp, bunkhouse, cookhouse, or warehouse. Usually about ten feet wide by twenty-five feet long, wanigans drew only inches of water. The bunk wanigan slept about twenty-five men. Another housed the cooks, cookees, their stoves, or supplies. In contrast, a bateau was a long, shallow-bottomed row or pole boat used to ferry men about the river, ride especially treacherous rapids, pick up supplies, and tow the wanigans across lakes or other still waters.

On the spring drives, men had to eat, sleep, and get dry when they could because the logs were moving come hell or high water. Usually a man got a snoose bag—a burlap or canvas sack full of a day's worth of food—from the cook in the morning and carried it with him because it might be impossible to get back to the wanigans at mealtime. The foreman divided the river into sections, or beats, making a crew responsible for each. Sometimes a driver, or river pig, went a day or two ahead of the wanigan and positioned himself at some especially difficult rapids or bend in the river, where he worked to keep the logs moving and to avoid a logjam. Men also had to travel ahead to open or close dams, raising water levels in the river as logs came down. Sluices had to be monitored and each log fed through the gates with a pike pole so they would not jam. Many of the men traveled on shore, walking gig trails worn along the riverbanks from one beat camp to the next. Some made their way downriver on the logs themselves. Many worked from a bateau.

Timber cruisers like Whiteside noted the best means of transportation for a given stand of pine on the same trip in which they located that pine. Typically they suggested a strategy and noted good sites for camps, roads, dams, or other river improvements, and from these notes the foreman made his plans. The summer before he went after a stand the logging foreman sent crews to the area to make the dams and other river improvements needed to raise water levels enough to float the logs out the following spring. These crews used timber cut near the site, hauled rocks from the shores of rivers to fill cribs, and cobbled together the dams and sluiceways, using heavy pieces such as pulleys, gears, and gates that had arrived by sleigh the winter before. The jacks built as many types of dams as there were types of rivers, and, like the jacks themselves, the dams were functional, ingenious, and low mainte-nance. They built wing dams—log- and earth-filled walls leaning into the river current at about forty-five degrees—which focused both wa-ter and logs into a deeper channel. Or, if the dam was temporary, the jacks simply laid logs across a river's bottom to raise the water level. The dams at the outlets of lakes were usually the largest and most carefully constructed in a transportation system, the water above the dam serv-ing as a log pond. A river jack, or catty man, rolled the logs over the top of the dam with a peavey, but sometimes the jacks blew a dam with dy-namite, sending an entire pondful of logs crashing downstream at once.[7]

Development of the transportation system was not without its dan-gers. During the construction of a portage between Bass and Low Lakes, the height of land between the lakes gave way. A forest service crew led by Adolph Dolenshak, who was in the area to cut portage trails, witnessed the disaster:

During the night the men were awakened by what they thought was thunder rumblings. Imagine their surprise when in the morning they found that the lake had gone, a lake that was about a mile wide and three miles in length. Mr. Dolenshak says that the larger fish of the lake got away with the rush of water but that thousands of small fry were left high and dry on the bottom of Bass Lake basin.[8]

USFS ranger Jack Valentine wrote about the far-reaching effects of the Bass Lake washout in a letter to historian Wes White in 1978:

As Low Lake was considerably lower than Bass lake the Oliver Mining Company at one time maintained a sluiceway for the log driving that followed the outlet into Low Lake. This was a distance of only a few hundred feet and the flowage from Bass Lake eventually washed it out causing the break thru and when it did, it traveled thru Low Lake, Low River, Range Lake and Range River into the lower end of Jackfish Bay on Basswood Lake. A tremendous amount of water went thru the area taking out trees and rocks as well as the railroad. There was debris hanging 20 to 30 feet in the remaining trees and it also took out a 1/2 mile or more of steel and ties on a curve taking it over the top of a spruce swamp standing it up like a fence.[9]

A prime danger during the spring drive, logjams were common and could be extremely impressive. The river pigs had to act quickly if logs began to hang up in the river, as more logs were continually coming down and adding to the mess. When the jam closed a river, logs stacked up for miles behind the snag, water flooded the banks upstream, and the pressure grew immense. The men carefully and slowly untangled the logs with peavey poles and screw jacks, always looking for that key log, the one thought to be the center of the jam.

When the logs reached the lakes, boom rats gathered them in corrals bounded by twenty-foot white pine trunks, their flattened ends augured with three-inch holes threaded with boom chain to hold the pine together. White pine logs, what the lumberjacks called "cork" pine, floated higher than any other species and were a convenient tool for gathering the other logs. As booms filled, a tug, alligator, or horse head works hauled the huge rafts across the lake to mill or hoist. Winton lumberjack Matt Laitala described work on a tug with Jim Gates, a hard-fighting, fierce-swearing, bandy-legged jack:

> One time we got to hauling some boom sticks down to the end of the lake, just two side by side, and we were going to set the sticks again for the next raft. We made the turn between the islands, and the boom sticks got stuck on the shore of the island. He says, "Go

*A logjam's immensity could be breathtaking, logs stacked up for miles,*
*the river impassable, the work of untangling it fraught with danger.*
*This jam was photographed on the Little Fork River in Koochiching County in 1937,*
*the last log drive in Minnesota.*

back there and push those damn sticks off!" Some of those boom
sticks were pretty small on the end so if you stepped on the end
you'd sink a little bit. I pushed those sticks while he kept pulling
with the tug and when they had cleared shore I jumped on to the
last ones and started up toward the tug with my pike pole in my
hand, walking on the sticks. He was waiting a little bit and the boom
sticks had kind of sagged a little bit—they weren't in a straight line.
He saw me out there coming along on those things and all of a sudden, he let that tug go; by starting out and pulling those sticks
straight . . . hoping I would lose my balance and go into the lake.[10]

These logging rafts could be hundreds of feet across, a challenge to
tow through the many islands and reefs without hitting a snag. If Minnesota is the land of ten thousand lakes, it is the land of thirty thousand
islands. But perhaps a bigger problem was wind. A good tail wind could
carry a boom and tug down the lake and make easy work. However, a
strong tail wind could swing a boom out to one side of the tug, almost
overtaking it, while a quartering wind pulled the boom and tug sideways, forcing the whole load to crab down the lake. Worse, a steady
head wind stopped all action, for even the best tugs could not pull a
large log raft into the wind.

In lakes that were too inaccessible for a tug to reach, the jacks used
a bull of the woods or alligator, a flat-bottomed scow with a steam-
powered drum mounted on its deck. The drum carried up to a mile of
cable, its running end spliced to a thousand-pound anchor. The alligator went out ahead of the logs, dropped anchor, and then reeled out
the cable as it made its way back to the boom. Boom men hooked the
'gator onto a full boom, throttled the steam engine, reeled in the cable,
and towed the logs across the lake. Even in the heaviest winds the
'gator and boom could not be blown off course farther than the cable's
length. The 'gator was so powerful it could pull itself across short
portages, shallows, and reefs.[11]

On smaller lakes the jacks built a crab on site and used horses for
power. These large structures, usually forty to eighty feet long, were
made of heavy timbers flattened on one side to create a level deck on
which the jacks mounted a drum winch wound with a heavy rope. A

bateau or sacking boat ran an anchor out ahead of the crab, and then two horses harnessed to a long capstan turned the drum, wound in the rope, and dragged the rig up to its anchor. Crabs were more susceptible to heavy wind, so when the weather was right the crews worked around the clock. Both men and horses lived in shelters on the decks of these boats.[12]

Once the logs were delivered to the millpond, most of the jacks were out of work until the next year. Many, especially teamsters, went back to farms or found work on the Dakota wheat fields. A few got jobs in the mill for the summer run; some began building next winter's camps, dams, and roads. However, most jacks, in town for the first time in nine or ten months, had other things on their minds than dams, camps, farms, or wheat fields. Their focus was threefold: women, whiskey, and fights.

It was said a lumberjack would eat a bale of hay if someone sprinkled whiskey on it. While not all jacks were drunks, the randy behavior of those who were built a well-deserved reputation for the entire group. Whorehouses were just one common and well-established tradition in the lumberjack life. Lumberjack queens followed the pine and set up shop near sawmills—in effect operating the new town's first business—or along the skid rows or trails in the woods, although bosses were careful not to let them get too close to camps. So established was this enterprise that the Western Michigan Whore Association actually unionized prostitution.[13]

As townsfolk moved into the area, following on the heels of the lumberjack and his women, they organized town councils and established law and order, forcing most of the whorehouses to relocate just outside city limits. This was the case in Ely, where some of the houses were set up along the skid rows or on the east end of Shagawa Lake near the settlement called Sibley. In the smaller towns there often was livery service from the saloons to the whorehouses: the saloonkeepers loaded the jacks into the wagon and pointed the horse toward its destination, and when the queens wanted to get rid of the lumberjacks they sent the horse and its wagonload back to town.[14]

Like many of the men, these women were often the disenfranchised of society, alcoholics or addicts, born to poverty, unlucky immigrants with few other options. Usually these houses were run by a madam and kept somewhat respectable. But sometimes the business practices were more ominous:

> The keeper of a resort at Ely . . . bought the girl for $50. Only 19 years of age and a widow seven months after her marriage, she was induced to go to Ely by promises of plenty of work . . . in the hotels and stores of that place. [She] sobbingly told the entire story of her seduction and imprisonment in the disorderly resort on the road between Ely and Winton.
>
> She asserts that when she got off the train at Ely the party was taken at once to the house in the wilderness. Once inside, the man who deceived her is said to have told the housekeeper to fit her out with a house gown. That same night she told police that she was forced to submit to outrageous indignities.

This house seems to have been particularly notorious: "Lumberjack Stony Slim, who had lost an eye in the woods, or fighting, was sitting in the girlie house when someone shot through a window and killed him . . . in his good eye, the story went."[15]

Horrified by the shootings, kidnappings, brawls, and other problems, townspeople found ways to limit the lumberjacks' sprees. Today, Tower, a town that in its heyday reportedly had close to one hundred saloons, has only one full-service saloon within city limits, located downstairs from city hall. As the cut continued, boomtowns developed into established cities and towns. Their respectable institutions like churches and schools left little room for the trailblazers and loggers who had made settlement possible.

# 5

## Labor in the Northland

*Long-haired preachers come out every night,*
*Try to tell you what's wrong and what's right;*
*But when asked how 'bout something to eat*
*They will answer with voices so sweet:*
*"You will eat, bye and bye,*
*In that glorious land above the sky;*
*Work and pray, live on hay,*
*You'll get pie in the sky when you die."*

    JOE HILL, "The Preacher and the Slave"

---

AMERICAN IDEALS underwent a profound metamorphosis and re-organization as the twentieth century approached. Laissez faire fell from favor. In addition to revised policies regarding disposal of the public domain, lumbermen on the Winton watershed had to contend with a changing labor situation. Despite the largest social aid program in American history—the Homestead Act and other land giveaways—the American dream had eluded many. The founding fathers had seen the value in making land available for settlement: Thomas Jefferson believed a country of landed farmers would form the best democracy; the practical and elite John Adams acknowledged that "power always followed property." But for some that vision had never materialized. A miserable, landless underclass, a population ruled by the pitiless marketplace, grew in both size and discontent until it threatened the peace.

On July 17, 1877, railroad workers in West Virginia went on strike against the Baltimore and Ohio Railroad after the company slashed their wages. To fight the strikers, the company hired the Pinkerton Detective Agency, a Civil War–era anti-espionage organization, its tactics aggressive and violent. Workers traveling the rail lines from city to city carried word of the Pinkertons' abuse, and solidarity spread, fire-like, from the railroad yards to workers in other industries, inspiring a general strike that soon extended coast to coast. A rally for the Working Man's Party in Chicago drew twenty thousand attendees, and public opinion seemed to be with the strikers. After the state militia refused to fire on the disgruntled workers, President Rutherford B. Hayes sent in federal troops. The resulting bloody conflict launched the modern labor movement in the United States.

The terrible and inhumane living conditions of the masses contrasted sharply with the opulence emerging industrialists and financiers enjoyed. Calls for action were wrapped up in issues of class—the haves versus the have nots—and questions of responsibility—that of business owners and of the government. Jacob Riis published *How the Other Half Lives* in 1890, shocking the nation with descriptions and photographs of the slums in New York City. In 1904, Henry James described the United States as a "huge Rappacini garden, rank with each variety of the poison-plant of the money passion." Jack London published *The Iron Heel* in 1906. These works powerfully illustrated the desperate conditions so many Americans suffered and forcibly demanded that those in power respond.[1]

Progressive journalists, seeking to mimic the financial success of Upton Sinclair's *The Jungle,* an exposé of the meatpacking industry published in 1906, took aim at business and political corruption, child labor, slum conditions, racial discrimination, prostitution, sweatshops, insurance fraud, environmental degradation, and illegal stock fixing. *Colliers, McClure's,* and *Atlantic Monthly* published well-researched features about a plethora of social scandals and injustices, a new activist journalism branded "muckraking" by President Theodore Roosevelt. Despite the unappealing appellation, muckrakers successfully galvanized public opinion and forced reform, the earliest examples being the Pure Food and Drug Act and the Meat Inspection Act, passed by Congress just six months after *The Jungle*'s publication.

As the press excoriated deplorable working conditions and exposed instances of business corruption, workers slowly began exercising their strength in numbers. Organizations like the Farmer-Labor Party in Minnesota, the Greenback Labor Party, grange societies, and other farmers' and laborers' unions formed to promote government ownership of the railroads and utilities, a graduated income tax, the secret ballot, women's suffrage, prohibition of alcohol, and federal regulation of inflation and the economy. In the 1890s there were about a thousand strikes each year; by 1904, four thousand. Many Americans, especially immigrants from northern Europe, where socialism was well established, adopted and promoted socialistic ideals and policies as they sought parity with employers. Northern Minnesota's workforce—numbering 15,886 just after the turn of the century—was particularly ripe for labor organization. The saw log harvest was mostly over, the big tree jacks having already migrated west, leaving behind second-growth or pulp loggers, gyppos, many of them paid for each log cut. Life in the camps and in the woods during the industrial phase was far different from that of the pioneer phase, with draconian conditions rampant under the new forest products syndicate.[2]

Company scalers often cheated the immigrant gyppos. Very few made the traditional pay scale of a dollar a day plus room and board; worse, many companies began charging gyppos for their keep. Employment agencies bid down wages and forced workers to compete against each other for jobs. Camp and mill foremen often charged new employees a hiring fee, using this money to pay the "man catcher" who had brought in the "recruit," a portion of the fee kicked back to the foreman. Since most jacks had no money when they arrived in camp, the company forced them to work off the hiring fee, adding to their initial debt daily board charges, hospitalization fees, tool rental fees, and outstanding wanigan balances. Some men worked an entire season only to discover that they owed the company money at spring thaw. Unscrupulous foreman fired workers as they fulfilled their monetary obligations and brought in new men to begin the cycle of indebtedness.[3]

Once men joined a camp they were at the mercy of the company. One worker reported an especially insidious form of control used on the men, addiction: "They have deliberately cultivated the narcotic drug habit among the workers. At every company store, cocaine, morphine and heroin are sold. The workers, once addicted, cannot think of going away from their source of supply, even if they could scrape together enough money to pay for the journey." While this observer was reporting on conditions in the Pacific Northwest, narcotic use also occurred at the camps in the Ely area. J. C. "Buzz" Ryan, local logger and historian, remembered, "One of the big sellers in the camps was 'toothache' medicine, little bottles of laudanum," a powerful and highly addictive drug.[4]

Industry mostly frustrated worker attempts to fight against these devious policies until 1905, when William Haywood, leader of the Western Federation of Miners, met with a crowd of socialists, anarchists, trade unionists, and revolutionaries in Chicago's Brand's Hall. The barrel-chested "Big Bill" called the meeting to order by hammering the front table with a plank. "Fellow Workers," he bellowed, "this is the Continental Congress of the Working Class. We are here to confederate the workers of this country into a working-class movement in possession of the economic power, the means of life, in control of the machinery of production and distribution without regard to capitalist masters." So began the first sermon of what writer and environmentalist Wallace Stegner termed the "militant church." To the Industrial Workers of the World (IWW), the Promised Land was nothing less than worldwide equality through total social and economic revolution.[5]

Unlike other labor unions, which usually focused their energy on a single trade, the IWW hoped to organize all workers from all industries into one big union, beginning with those who had the least power and suffered most: women, blacks, immigrants, migrant workers, loggers. By organizing across industries the world over, the IWW sought to erase the division between capital and labor. Haywood's 1914 stationery expressed the IWW philosophy: "It is the historic mission of the working class to do away with capitalism. By organizing industrially we are forming the structure of the new society within the shell of the old."

Many agreed with this sentiment, and workers flocked to the "Wobbly" banner.[6]

The IWW organized loggers in the Pacific Northwest in 1907. Their demands were straightforward enough: an eight-hour work day, Sundays and holidays off, higher wages, good food served in clean porcelain instead of greasy tin, no overcrowding at the dining tables, sanitary kitchens, no more than twelve men to a bunkhouse and one man to a bunk, spring cots, blankets, showers, free hospital service, and semi-monthly pay by bank check instead of time scrip. Most companies paid the lumberjacks in time checks, redeemable at the company office only after receipts from that year's lumber sales had been paid. Often jacks waited for their money in logging towns full of expensive temptations and perilous chance designed to separate a man from his check. Every saloon, almost all stores, some boarding houses, and even banks cashed time checks, always for a percentage on the dollar. In Minnesota, many jacks rode the rails out of town flat broke, bound for work in the Dakota wheat fields only days after cashing their time check at a brass rail or bordello. In the Dakotas they worked the threshers, making their way back to the lumber camps as the snow fell.[7]

Disenfranchised and transient, moving in and out of the industry as their wallets demanded, loggers were obvious candidates for IWW membership. As a group, few had suffered more at the hands of industry, and it was no surprise that the jacks took the Wobbly message of equality, respect, and strength and made it their own. Their transience allowed them freedom to organize workers across large areas, and for those men without families—in 1900, 56 percent of lumberjacks were single— company starve-out tactics were less successful. Most important, years of terrible treatment had galvanized their anger into resolve, making lumberjacks determined organizers.[8]

The jacks' resolve notwithstanding, lumber companies were formidable opponents. Typically, the sawmill was the town's largest business. In Winton, for example, St. Croix and Swallow and Hopkins owned the majority of the town's real estate and controlled most of the surrounding countryside. The companies owned the stores, the fire-fighting equipment, the municipal heating system, water system, and electrical plant. Company managers and officers were also town bureaucrats who ran everything save the post office. Out in the woods the loggers were isolated and divided at the remote camps, far removed from witnesses or media that might authenticate any violent incidents and sway public opinion.

In Minnesota, ɪww struggles began in the mining industry but soon spread to the lumber mills and logging camps. With their ties to northern Europe, many of the immigrant jacks carried strong family traditions of unionism and socialism. The Finnish, especially, were more socially liberal and better organized than other groups on the range. In June 1913, local Finns incorporated the Winton Finnish Socialist Association, defining the group's purpose as "[the promotion of] morals and the education of its members in political and economic matters and diffusion of such knowledge among the people." To this end, they built the Finnish Hall, organized an athletic club, held dances, and started a library. And soon there was a strike at the St. Croix mill, reported in the *Ely Miner:*

> The Finnish speaking dry lumber pilers and trim men of the St. Croix Lbr. & Mfg. Co. went out on a strike Monday morning without first preparing to arbitrate with the superintendent of the company which might have been done under the circumstances, but instead of so doing, went out blank spank which caused the mill to shut down. The mill was shut down up to Thursday afternoon when they started to operate the day shift. The strikers offered to go back to work for a 10 cent raise which was refused by the Supt. About 60 to 70 men are involved and of that amount the larger part can be replaced by men shipped in. Very few of the old crew is being put to work. It is expected that by the first of the week both shifts will be working.

Other labor efforts in Winton seemed to be equally ineffective. In August 1915, Tom Whitten and other St. Croix managers stopped a group of strikers on their way to the mill, Whitten indicating that he would ignore any demands and fire outright any man who struck. None did.[9]

Other labor conflicts were more pedestrian. Lumberjack Matt Laitala recalled one strike at the Swallow and Hopkins Horse Lake Camp:

The boss put the handyman into the kitchen . . . that handyman had been in camp 13 months without taking a bath, and his arms— I remember the skinny bugger, he was an old white haired, long-hair—and . . . his arms . . . were . . . crusted with dirt! Black John, who was the boss of the camp, opened that barn door at the end of the camp and said, "Well let's try 'er again, eh, boys?" and nobody moved. So he came back, looking like he thought he hadn't said it loud enough, and says, "Let's fire it up, boys!" Nobody moved. He came in and said, "What's the matter fellas?" One of the Finn guys said, "No eat, no work!" And it wasn't long before we got another cook. The lumberjacks didn't know how long this damn handyman was going to be messin' around in the kitchen, so they weren't going to put up with it.[10]

In the rest of the state, few lumber strikes were resolved as reasonably. The Wobblies organized workers from Virginia, Bemidji, Duluth, Gemmell, and Monticello up to International Falls, from the northern counties of Koochiching, Itasca, St. Louis, and Beltrami all the way down to Wright County just south of Minneapolis. In the Brainerd, Crookston, and International Falls areas, Backus-Brooks, the Virginia and Rainy Lake Company, and Crookston Lumber, run by Sam Simpson, the first contract logger for Swallow and Hopkins, fought repeated strikes. Thugs beat and jailed Wobblies or simply loaded them at gunpoint onto trains to be shipped out of the state; lumber companies pursued IWW organizers, broke up meetings, intimidated members.[11]

By the end of 1916, the State of Minnesota had so much labor trouble that it appropriated fifty thousand dollars to investigate matters in its lumbering camps and mining towns. But before anything could be resolved, in 1917 the Wobblies managed to organize a strike against lumber companies across northern Minnesota. A supporter of the timber industry, Governor John Lind asked the legislature to send in the state militia and called for federal troops to "protect the property" of the lumber companies. Backus-Brooks and Virginia and Rainy Lake brought in Pinkertons; company and state police joined with local law enforcement to beat, jail, and blacklist the Wobblies. The fighting spilled out of the woods and mills and into the towns, whose residents, tending to favor labor, joined in the demonstrations, compelling the companies to call in more sheriffs and unofficial deputies for protection.[12]

The Minnesota legislature hastily formed a committee on labor, which sent out almost one hundred subpoenas to those in all ranks and, on January 30, 1917, began open-session hearings in an attempt to reconcile timber workers and the lumber companies. The inexperienced committee bickered relentlessly regarding protocol in the tense, hot, overcrowded court full of competing interests—defensive employers, aggressive and militant unionists, fearful and angry workers, even shameful scabs, all corralled in one miserable room.

The first to take the stand was a native of Brooklyn and a bachelor, twenty-five years old, an employee of Backus-Brooks International Lumber Company in Bemidji. Arthur W. Thorne had been persuaded by fellow Wobblies to organize jacks in the Gemmell and International Falls area. Thorne testified that Backus-Brooks sent sheriffs and deputies into the camps to maintain order, that Pinkertons and sheriffs opened the men's mail, that they used intimidation tactics, saying they had orders to "shoot to kill" any who participated in organizing activities. Still, a camp in Gemmell organized, and Thorne gave the foreman a list of demands, asking "to have the bunk house scrubbed out twice a week and to have clean bedding, and to get a pay day twice a month," emphasizing "the main thing . . . better food, and sanitary food." When the foreman's response was to fire the workers, every camp in Gemmell closed up the next day. Thorne reported, "the sheriff took me off the train between Northome and Gemmell and throwed me in jail," charged with riot.[13]

Efforts to crush the loggers were intense and widespread, and still the Wobblies persisted, talking one man or woman to another, gathering in small groups, organizing across the country. It was difficult to fight the iww, but anti-union forces went after the group aggressively. Just half a year after Big Bill Haywood's legendary meeting in Chicago, authorities arrested him and other iww leaders for the murder of anti-union ex-governor of Idaho, Frank Steunenberg, who was killed by a bomb. Clarence Darrow represented the Wobblies and exposed the state's main witness as a perjurer. The jury found the iww innocent.

Prosecuting attorney and later senator William Borah voiced his frustration in trying the IWW: "you cannot destroy the organization. . . . It is something you cannot get at. You cannot reach it. You do not know where it is. It is not in writing. It is not in anything else. It is a simple understanding between men, and they act upon it without any evidence of existence whatever." This grassroots aspect of the IWW was not premeditated but an organic fact, as recalled by members years later: "We also said we had no leaders. We meant just that. That didn't mean we didn't recognize that someone might be a better speaker or organizer or better at this or that, but they had no authority. No one ever sent an IWW anywhere to do anything."[14]

Interest in unions grew after the stock market crashed in 1929, as suddenly many more Americans could relate to the plight of the poor— the pains of hunger, the injustices faced by the working class. This widespread intimacy with injustice bred activism, and pervasive grassroots activism brought change. The organization of repressed peoples against injustice was a natural force, unavoidable, immutable, uncontrollable.

In Minnesota, the Gemmell strike eventually collapsed, but the Wobblies and their message proved difficult to eradicate. Stating succinctly why IWW membership continued to grow despite powerful opposition, worker Irving Hanson said he joined in 1919 because "it seemed a logical answer to a rather troubled world."[15]

Many managers came to believe that no amount of repression could end union activity. They saw that the more aggressive their efforts, the more resolved the workers. Additionally, they felt the tide of public opinion turning against them. Some of the most prominent industrial and labor figures of the day began looking for an alternative. Republican and conservative Ralph Easley, Marcus A. Hanna, head of the Republican Party, Andrew Carnegie, industrialist John D. Rockefeller Jr., and Samuel Gompers, head of the American Federation of Labor (AFL) formed the National Civic Federation in 1900. By supporting conservative labor organizations like Gompers's, industrialists marginalized the more demanding and, to their purposes, more dangerous Wobblies. For its part, the IWW labeled Gompers a "labor faker" and "pie card artist."[16]

In Minnesota, the jacks and other workers were not the only population facing unfair treatment from the lumber companies, whose abandoned cutover lands caused grave economic deprivation for the state's citizens. The companies had long placated locals by claiming that the cleared forests would become farmland, opening opportunities for a new local industry. Some companies published flyers in Italian, French, German, and other languages touting the newly cleared land to lure overseas buyers. While this pattern had played out in the East, where pioneers turned many forests to farms, the same was not true in northern Minnesota, where the glacial soils are thin, sandy, and acidic, fine for pine trees but inhospitable to food crops, and where wolves, cougars, foxes, wolverines, and other predators, along with brutal temperatures, made husbandry difficult. Average yearly farm income on the Arrowhead between 1924 and 1935 was about $335, paltry compared to the statewide average of $1,371. Many farmers worked winters in the woods to make their farms pay; they knew the conditions in the camps intimately. Not surprisingly, the timber industry enjoyed only ragged support on the range.[17]

At the beginning of the 1935 logging season, workers at the Minnesota and Ontario Paper Company went on a wildcat strike, petitioning the American Federation of Labor for backing. The strike failed, but the AFL granted the jacks a charter to form Local 2776 of the Timber Workers Union, a subsidiary of the United Brotherhood of Carpenters and Joiners. The following year, organizers for Local 2776 developed support in a number of the larger northern camps. After talking with membership, they presented two companies that operated some of northern Minnesota's largest camps, General Logging and International Lumber, with a list of demands: four dollars for an eight-hour day, no more than a dollar a day fee for bunk and board, single instead of double bunks, shower houses and washtubs in all camps, payroll twice monthly in U.S. currency rather than company time checks, and union recognition. The company refused all demands. Jacks near Lake Vermilion struck: within two days 2,500 men were out across the northland, and by the end of the week union membership had swelled to four thousand. The burr of crosscut saws faltered, then fell silent across Minnesota for the first time in almost one hundred years.[18]

In 1917 Governor Lind had helped crush the Wobblies, but times and the political climate had changed. Farmer-Labor Governor Elmer Benson promised to have a State Industrial Commission representative investigate any attempt at strike breaking. He also offered state relief and ordered the National Guard and highway patrol to assist the strikers. As supplies in the camps ran low, loggers straggled into town. Winton's Finnish Hall became a union meeting place and a home for striking workers, and the Duluth armory sheltered homeless jacks, members of the National Guard distributing blankets and clothing. Support for the strikers was widespread and robust. When International Lumber tried

*Like their Minnesota counterparts, timber workers on strike near Marenisco, Michigan, in 1937 sought improved working conditions and fair pay.*

to lock out timber workers and hire area farmers, the farmers over-whelmingly endorsed the union. Unable to break the strike, industry negotiators offered a compromise one-year agreement. Local 2776 accepted. The strike was over: the workers had won.

Their victory was short-lived, however, for International Lumber's stunning loss galvanized solidarity in the industry. The following summer timber companies, fierce adversaries for decades, formed the Minnesota Timber Producers Association (MTPA). With over 85 percent of Minnesota's timber production accounted for in this group, MTPA leaders knew a unified front and single negotiating body would mount an effective defense of industry interests. Indeed, the organization was, and has remained, remarkably successful at fighting lumber's battles against labor organization, bureaucratic regulation, and environmental reform.

In October 1937 the MTPA proposed a contract that eliminated many of the hard-won concessions of the previous year. Within a few days over four thousand timber workers went on strike. The MTPA launched a sophisticated media campaign, promoting the idea that labor had rejected a reasonable contract, telling the *Duluth News Tribune* that they had offered workers a 33 percent wage increase. Union organizers pointed out that four-fifths of the workers were gyppos, paid by the cut, and the wage increase applied only to foremen, cooks, and clerks, not to the lumberjacks. Further, they argued, "We had such slavery conditions to come up from that percentages of increases are meaningless. The fact is that the timber barons, who have made millions upon millions of dollars by robbing Minnesota of its forests, are forcing us to strike because they refuse to pay a wage of 40 to 42 and 1/2 cents an hour."[19]

Addressing a group that had previously sided against logging companies—northern farmers—the MTPA suggested that the union threatened their livelihoods, reasoning that, if the industry was forced to shut down, the result would be no winter work for struggling farmers and a smaller market for their goods. An MTPA handbill urged "all farmers, who sell timber products or work in the woods . . . to fight the racketeers who would keep us from making a living." However, most farmers remained loyal to the striking loggers. A group of eighty-two sent Governor Benson a letter declaring, "we . . . have discussed the timber workers strike and feel that their demands are just and we are ready to help them out in every possible way."[20]

On June 17, 1937, the Minnesota State Board of Health intervened on behalf of the loggers, publishing a seventeen-page manual of regulations covering everything from the sites on which a camp could be built, to the size of bunkhouses (at least 300 cubic feet of air space for every inhabitant), to toilets and washing, bathing, and laundering facilities, to medical service and the dimensions of blankets. With this official policy, the old-style, rough shanty camp became a thing of history.

The union eventually won many of its demands for reasonable pay and decent accommodations, but it could not overcome fifty years of overharvest. The last log drive in the state, on the Little Big Fork River, was in 1937. There was no pine left to cut. Wildfires had made natural regeneration marginal, and tree-planting efforts were in their infancy. Lumber companies continued to leave for the forests of the South or the Pacific Northwest. Forest service logging roads allowed men to get to a jobsite without having to live in camps, while increased mechanization eliminated many jobs. The loggers who remained in northern Minnesota were mostly local men, part of small family crews running independent operations—Cyrille Fortier, Harry Homer, Jacob Pete, and the Kainz brothers—cutting pulp off private holdings or off the national forest for the large paper mills in Cloquet, Duluth, and International Falls. These crews had little need for labor organization: Jacob Pete scorned the Wobblies, claiming IWW stood for "I Won't Work," "I Want Women," or "I Want Whiskey."[21]

To a large degree, once the pine was gone, unionism in northern Minnesota's lumber industry was moot. Today the MTPA has sold its agenda to the remaining contract operators who cut the meager aspen that grew in the wake of the pine; the loggers and truck drivers, the jacks, now give teeth to MTPA opposition to environmental efforts aimed at reestablishing big pine on the Arrowhead. The association's executive director, Wayne Brandt, sits on the Minnesota Forest Resources Council. The MTPA website promotes industry interests, offering educational materials to loggers, private landowners, and schools. Brandt describes MTPA's current membership as "loggers, truckers, small sawmills and allied businesses throughout Minnesota" and explains its mission: "MTPA represents its members in local, state and national forums on legislative and regulatory issues." Today, labor and management are mostly united under the MTPA because the labor force has been largely eliminated. Small, independent contractors with heavy machinery have replaced the army of jacks, an "every worker for himself" model that renders unionism unnecessary and erases the line between workers and owners.[22]

# 6

## Conservation Gains Traction

*It is our manifest destiny to overspread and to possess the whole of the continent which Providence has given us for the development of the great experiment of liberty and federated self government entrusted to us.*

JOHN L. O'SULLIVAN, editor, *New York Post*, 1845[1]

---

THE INDUSTRIAL PHASE OF LAND USE drew to a close as the large timber companies pulled out of the northland, leaving in their wake collapsed tax rolls, shuttered mills, widespread unemployment, and ravaging wildfire. The next phase, conservation, was an attempt to mitigate these many evils. The seeds of conservation had been planted years earlier, in the East, where forests were long gone. Conservation was a reaction to perceived dearth, to impending timber famine. This movement marked the end of a unique American belief in the continent's boundless resources.

On July 12, 1893, University of Wisconsin history professor Frederick Jackson Turner read a paper at the Columbian Exposition in Chicago. In the newly erected marbled halls of a faux Grecian monument, what would later become the Art Institute, Turner declared the great American frontier closed:

> What the Mediterranean . . . was to the Greeks, breaking the bond of custom, offering new experiences, calling out new institutions

and activities, that, and more, the ever retreating frontier has been
to the United States. . . . And now, four centuries from the discovery of America, at the end of a hundred years of life under the
Constitution, the frontier has gone, and with its going has closed
the first period of American history.

Turner's first major paper made a dramatic impression, describing as it
did a nameless angst that many of his American contemporaries
shared. While the concept of an actual frontier—a line of settlement
that began in the east and progressed across the continent from the Atlantic toward the Pacific—was far too simplistic, Americans had long
responded to the notion as if it were fact. With the central organizing
principle of American society, namely, the settlement of the continent,
dissolved, the nation cast about without direction.[2]

Fundamental ideas wrapped up in the American notion of frontier—the divine right to expand and overtake new territory, the in-
exhaustibility of natural resources, the rightness of American progress,
the opportunity afforded any rugged individual—all of these and more
were proving increasingly untenable. While the geographic premise
of Turner's thesis was strained, he managed to touch upon a real truth:
the frontier as he and other Americans had understood it was indeed
defunct. Mounting numbers of citizens looked to the future with
dread, not hope. The availability of seemingly endless, unknown, unexplored, and unclaimed tracts had almost guaranteed liberty for the
colonists. Horace Greeley's siren song, "Go West, young man, and
grow up with the land," described a broad social safety net. This net
had been unraveling for some time before Turner called people's attention to it.

Twenty years before the Columbian Exposition some of the nation's
most influential thinkers began predicting a timber famine; by the time
Turner read his paper their concerns were gaining traction. At the turn
of the century, the conversion of natural resources had been industrialized, the rate of exploitation growing exponentially. The government
hemorrhaged land during the nineteenth century, transferring almost
one-half from federal ownership to state or private hands but seeing
much of it returned via tax forfeiture within decades. Worse, by 1893

four-fifths of the nation's timber had been consumed by the highly integrated, well-capitalized, and mechanically industrialized corporations that devoured the enormous forests of the Great Lakes. For the first time, the environmental consequences of Manifest Destiny weighed heavily on the collective American consciousness.[3]

One possible solution to the dwindling resource base was also on display at the 1893 World's Fair, as described in the fair guide:

> The forest resources of the world are exhibited in the Forestry
> Building, which is one of the most interesting and unique struc-
> tures on the grounds. It is made of wood and has a colonnade com-
> posed of tree trunks sent from almost every state in the Union.
> For instance, California sent sugar pine, redwood and trunks of
> the young sequoia; Minnesota, white pine, sugar maple, ash, oak,
> cottonwood, spruce, box cedar, tamarack and elm.[4]

While many of the milling and tree displays were sponsored by companies set on glorifying the logging industry, there were two important exceptions. Young Gifford Pinchot, recently returned from studying forestry in Europe, manned a booth sponsored by George Vanderbilt's Biltmore Estate. In 1892, at the recommendation of Frederick Law Olmstead, designer of New York's Central Park, Vanderbilt hired Pinchot as head forester on his twenty-thousand-acre estate. His work there was the nation's first practical expression of the science of forestry. The second was Bernard Fernow, head of the newly created Division of Forestry, whose booth was most likely located in the U.S. Government Building. The two, Pinchot and Fernow, promoted the ideas of silviculture and managed forestry: that trees could be grown just like corn or beans, that forest fires were wasteful and destructive, that tree planting was a civic duty, that science could succeed in averting the predicted timber famine.

The theme of the 1893 World's Fair was "Century of Progress," its appropriate focus the wonders of emerging technology. Perhaps its astonishing success—attendance was nearly 27 million, about 25 percent of the nation's population—was due to the antidote it offered to the national angst Turner had noted. The remarkable devices showcased at the Columbian Exposition—the telephones, engines, and phonographs, the first elevated electric railway, the moving sidewalks (which carried riders at six miles per hour), Gray's Teleautograph (a device that electrically reproduced handwriting), Thomas Edison's Kinetograph (a precursor to the movie projector), and wondrous electric lights that illuminated the fairgrounds at night—bolstered hope in endless possibilities. Some of America's most beloved foods—Cracker Jack, Aunt Jemima syrup, Cream of Wheat, Juicy Fruit gum, Pabst beer, diet carbonated soda, and the hamburger—were introduced at the Columbian Exposition. Change, innovation, and progress became America's banners, defining the country's self-image for many years following the fair.

These wonders replaced the hope once afforded by an unexplored, unexploited continent. Mechanization and invention promised to provide more leisure, more beauty, and more safety; social scientists to alleviate class friction; biologists to find cures for pressing diseases like polio, typhoid, and staph; engineers to replace wood-fired steam engines with the internal combustion engine, thereby saving vast expanses of forest. And Pinchot and Fernow believed that scientific management of the nation's trees would provide a steady stream of products without destroying the forests and watersheds, that logging towns need not be boomtowns but places of employment across generations. The problem was time. If quick action were not taken to halt the environmental destruction accelerating across the continent, there would be little forest left for the new foresters to manage.

The philosophical shift from the unregulated consumption of resources and land to conservation of those resources, suppression of fire, and long-term management of water, soil, timber, minerals, and game came with glacial slowness. Congress had created Fernow's tiny Department of Forestry only after many years of bitter struggle against well-organized and powerful opposition. Turner's speech and Pinchot and Fernow's displays merely marked the inevitability of these new attitudes: implementation was still more than a decade away.[5]

For years before the Columbian Exposition, progressive writers, journalists, clergymen, scientists, and other opinion makers, in ever-increasing numbers, united in condemning the many social ills brought on by unregulated capitalism and the integrated industrial economy, what some historians have referred to as the "incorporation of America." The calls for reform were quiet at first and came mostly from academic and scientific circles, but as conditions deteriorated other voices joined the chorus until its demands could not be ignored.

In 1849 the patent office urged the federal government to conserve the public's forests: "The waste of timber in the United States, to say nothing of firewood, will hardly be appreciated until our population reaches 50,000,000. Then the folly and shortsightedness of this age will meet with a degree of censure not pleasant to contemplate."[6]

George Perkins Marsh was one of the first people to study how humans were changing the environment of North America and the problems these changes might cause. In his seminal book, *Man and Nature,* published in 1864, Marsh declared that deforestation was responsible for the collapse of civilizations from the Mayans to the Mesopotamians, the Chinese to the Carthaginians, the Athenians to the English. He presented strong evidence that clearing forests, overgrazing, and uncontrolled wildfire had destroyed the utility of once-productive lands across the globe. His well-formed arguments found a wide audience.

Another of America's well-known naturalists, Increase Lapham, agreed with Marsh. Assistant surveyor of the Erie Canal and designer and builder of the Welland and Miami Canals, Lapham was chief geologist for the state of Wisconsin from 1873 to 1875, at the height of the state's pine-logging boom. Watching the forests being devoured by lumbermen and the seed stock torched by the inevitable firestorms, at mid-century Lapham wrote:

> Few persons . . . realize . . . the amount we owe to the native forests of our country for the capital and wealth our people are now enjoying . . . yet without the fuel, the buildings, the fences, furniture and [a] thousand utensils and machines of every kind, the principal materials for which are taken directly from the forests . . . we should be reduced to a condition of destitution . . . anyone who studies closely and carefully the elements that have contributed to that greatness will find cheap lumber and cheap fuel the greatest of all factors . . . cheap houses, cheap bread and cheap transportation for passengers and freights, are among the fundamental elements of a nation's

growth and prosperity. . . . A nation that produces the raw material for manufacture at low cost . . . which moves its people, its products and manufactures quickly and cheaply, is in the best position.

Lapham, like Marsh, noted that the rise and fall of many past civilizations paralleled the condition of their forests, and he reached the obvious conclusion: America destroyed its own forests at grave peril. The damage to forests during Lapham's lifetime was severe: Americans burned for fuel almost 5 billion cords of wood, the equivalent of two million square miles of forest, and cut for lumber twenty-five thousand square miles of wilderness. With each passing year the rate of deforestation only accelerated.[7]

Soon others joined Marsh and Lapham in clamoring for change. In 1855, Charles Sargent, a botanist and director of Harvard University's Arnold Arboretum, wrote the paramount silvicultural index of American forests, *The Woods of the United States: With an Account of Their Structure, Qualities, and Uses.* In 1880 he re-surveyed America's forests for the census and, alarmed by what he found, published ecological warnings in *Harper's New Monthly Magazine* and *North American Review.* Other articles detailed the nation's impending timber famine, the plunder of natural resources and abuses of land laws, and the corruption of government bodies regarding the public domain, particularly manipulations by ranchers, miners, lumbermen, and railroad barons. An October 1885 *Harper's* article stated: "Out of the possession of the government and into the hands of unscrupulous men the public lands are passing at a rate so extravagant in acreage and so insignificant in price as to give cause for alarm, and the subject demands investigation."[8]

Grim predictions multiplied and gained momentum; concurrently, the reliability and authority of the speakers increased. Commissioner of the General Land Office Joseph M. Wilson wrote in 1868, "in forty or fifty years our own forests [will] have disappeared and those of Canada [will] be approaching exhaustion." F. B. Hough, respected scientist from Lowe, New York, was one of the first to urge reform directly to Congress when, at the 1873 annual meeting of the American Association for the Advancement of Science (AAAS), he presented a paper entitled "On the Duty of Governments in the Preservation of Forests." After reemphasizing the history others before him had outlined, Hough suggested that Congress establish a committee to inform the legislature and state governments of the need for "cultivation, regulation, and encouragement" of America's forested lands. The AAAS acted on his recommendations, and in September 1875 a group of these forward thinkers formed the American Forestry Association in Chicago, then the epicenter of the world's largest lumber market. Their objective: to foster "all interests of forest planting and conservation on this continent."[9]

But the nation's first practical public expression of professional forestry began in Minnesota, a state whose citizens, awakening to a firsthand knowledge of the evils of over-harvest, were slowly coming to terms with the collapse of what had been their major cash crop, white pine trees. While in many areas of the East and Midwest farmers had moved into the newly cleared areas and contributed to flourishing local economies after the forests were gone, in the Minnesota pine belts thin glacial soils and harsh weather made for marginal farming. The land in northern Minnesota was best suited to growing trees, not crops, but any notions of a pine forest naturally regenerating in the cutovers had to be abandoned as fire swept across the defunct pineries and burned all the seed stock.

Minnesota congressman Mark Dunnell, chairman of the Public Lands Committee, wrote a rider to the Appropriations Act of August 15, 1876, providing two thousand dollars for forestry research, the first public money spent on forestry in U.S. history. Congress set out to find a man "of approved attainments, who is practically well acquainted with methods of statistical inquiry, and who has evinced an intimate acquaintance with questions relating to the national wants in regard to timber" and a variety of other forest-related topics including the effect of forests on climate and their preservation and renewal. F. B. Hough was the obvious candidate, and the next year he submitted the first official forestry report to Congress, in which he wrote: "The misfortune has been, that the clearing [of forests] was made without a thought as to the probable wants of the future . . . and as a consequence, the supplies have within a few years past been found scarce and their prices have advanced to a degree that it is sensibly felt by all classes of the population."[10]

Hough continued to receive funding from Congress, and he published a second report in 1880. The next year Congress gave his tiny agency five thousand dollars, granting it the title "Division of Forestry" and placing it within the Department of Agriculture. The infant unit almost lost its funding the very next year, but again Congressman Dunnell took the floor in its defense, saying:

the Census reports taken in 1880 and now being prepared will disclose some very interesting facts concerning the quantity of growing timber . . . there are sections within the country . . . where . . . the supply will be entirely exhausted within the next ten, twelve, or fourteen years. The time is not far off when the question of lumber supply will become a practical question affecting very many of the material interests of the country.

With this reminder, Congress increased the yearly appropriations for the Division of Forestry to seven thousand dollars.[11]

Because no U.S. schools offered courses on forestry, Hough went to Europe, where people had struggled with timber shortages for centuries. Few books were available on the subject, but in 1882 the Robert Clarke and Company published *Elements of Forestry,* the preface by Hough declaring, "this is, so far as we know, the first attempt to present, in our language, and in one volume, the subject of Forestry." Soon the University of Michigan and Iowa State University began offering silvicultural courses, but still there was no college expressly dedicated to this new science and no degree in forestry available in the United States. Most Americans viewed tree planting and fire suppression as European notions, activities for smaller, resource-poor countries. Bernard E. Fernow helped change that perception.

A student at the prestigious Prussian Forest Academy at Muenden, Fernow journeyed to Philadelphia in 1876 to observe the American centennial celebration and to attend the American Forestry Association meeting. Fernow seriously doubted, given the fractured nature of American politics, that an organized, centralized management of the nation's far-flung forests would ever become a reality, but, after earning his

American citizenship through marriage, he put forth great effort to that end. On March 15, 1886, President Grover Cleveland appointed him head of the Division of Forestry, where Fernow found he had little authority, few forests to oversee, and only a meager ten-thousand-dollar appropriation to fund the department.[12]

In 1898 Fernow left the impotent Division of Forestry to head Cornell University's new college of forestry. In a program textbook Fernow clearly stated the central problem with which any public land manager or conservationist must grapple, the seemingly immutable economic realities of resource management:

> In most cases it will be found that the busy competition of the present has a destructive tendency and leads to wasteful methods. . . . While forms of government may change, the organization, the state idea, promises to be permanent. This conception of the permanency of the state, the realization that it is not a thing of to-day and for a limited time, but forever, widens its functions and extends its sphere of action; for it is no longer to be regarded as merely the arbiter between its present members, but it becomes the guardian of its future members; government becomes the representative not only of present communal interests, but also of future interests as against those of the present. We do not create this special providence for the individual, but for society; the individual will have to work out his own salvation.[13]

While attempting to plan for the future, the Division of Forestry and Congress itself faced one of the strongest lobbying forces in the country. The lumbering industry had significant monies and connections at its disposal and gained power through alliance with the railroad industry; together they controlled the nation's forests. For a time the lumber barons successfully stymied almost all land reform legislation.

But, as the abuses became more and more outrageous and the destruction more startling and terrible, the industry's defense of the status quo lost both measure and weight. As more and more Americans became fearful of and angry at the destruction and theft of the public domain, industry lobbyists and constituent-minded legislators, especially from the western states, could no longer adequately defend their positions. Carl Schurz told the American Forestry Congress in 1889, "I saw timber thieves, not stealing single trees, but stealing whole forests. . . . I saw dozens and scores and hundreds of lumber mills working at full blast without a single stick of timber being manufactured in them that did not come from the public lands."[14]

Edward A. Bowers, a lawyer within the General Land Office, estimated that between 1881 and 1887 lumber barons had stolen more than $36 million worth of timber from the public domain, of which agents recovered only $478,000. The appropriations given to protect the government's timberlands could support only twenty-five agents who were expected to patrol over 70 million acres of the public timberlands—2.8 million acres each.[15]

About this time Gifford Pinchot became obsessed with a radical new idea, one he termed "conservation." He realized that all resources—water, soils, trees—were interrelated and could only be effectively managed, or conserved, by a single authority. Conservation did not imply preservation, for the science of forestry, in Pinchot's understanding, was the art of using resources without destroying them. But Pinchot understood that because forests were so much more diverse in character and topography than farms, containing not only timber but grasslands, watersheds, wildlife, and minerals, all of which were vital to the public welfare, and because trees were not limited to one growing season like corn but required hundreds or more, only a single agency with dominion over all the natural resources could conserve them effectively and ensure their availability for future generations. The major shift was departmental: forestry and conservation, Pinchot believed, were agricultural affairs—thus, the forested portions of the remaining public domain belonged within the Department of Agriculture, under the

*Gifford Pinchot was instrumental in popularizing the tenets of conservation and creating the U.S. Forest Service.*

management of trained foresters, not with the notoriously inadequate Department of the Interior, whose handling of the public land was, according to Pinchot, "scandalous."

Even as arguments for restraint and for changed policies grew in strength, Congress could not forge solidarity adequate for passing any land reform legislation. The Mississippi River geographically divided those who wanted conservation, mostly representatives from the cutover pineries in the East and the rapidly disappearing forests of the Great Lakes, from those who stubbornly clung to the promise of Manifest Destiny in the West. One hundred and fifty miles north of that river's headwaters, the Winton logging industry teetered atop the wall dividing the debate.

Just as the Knox mill was about to begin its first season's cut in Winton, Department of the Interior special agent Webster Eaton investigated the scope, type, and specifics of land fraud in the Duluth district. Eaton determined that, by using false homestead entries, perjured preemption claims, and bogus swampland designation, lumbermen had stolen at least 50 million board feet of logs from the public the previous year. He examined 36 claims without finding one legitimate settlement. The October 26, 1894, *Ely Times* reported: "a conservative estimate of the stealing during the past 35 years from school, educational and United States lands, the fraudulent disposition of swamp lands . . . in this state, amounts to the appalling total of $657,131,817.00."[16]

Beginning in the 1890s, lumbermen knew that the cut-and-run logging days were about to end, and they worked to forestall the inevitable while acquiring as much timber under the old rules as possible. With the preemption law, cash sale law, and auction system repealed by Congress, they focused their energies on the only remaining avenue, Lincoln's homestead law, which despite well-known abuse was so popular that conservationists had no hopes of changing or abolishing it. Under the Homestead Act, settlers in the Duluth district took eleven thousand acres in 1870 and nine thousand acres in 1880. But lumbermen claimed almost 63,000 acres as homesteads in 1890, 241,095 acres in 1892, and 300,038 acres in 1901. Investigator Eaton estimated that nine-tenths of the homestead filings at the Duluth Land Office were fraudulent.[17]

With evidence mounting, on March 3, 1891, after much agitation by Fernow and Secretary of the Interior John W. Nobel, a weary Congress read "An Act to Repeal Timber Culture Laws and for Other Purposes," an agricultural appropriations bill. Section 24 of the act allowed the following:

> That the President of the United States may, from time to time, set apart and reserve, in any State or Territory having public land and bearing forests, in any part of the public lands wholly or in part covered with timber or undergrowth, whether of commercial value or not, as public reservations, and the President shall, by public proclamation, declare the establishment of such reservations and the limits thereof.

This language had been thoroughly debated in preceding sessions, and, despite initial objections that the act gave the president too much power, the most important environmental bill in U.S. history went to the executive office for signature. President Benjamin Harrison exercised his new authority almost immediately by creating Yellowstone Park Timberland Reserve, protecting 1.2 million acres for future generations. Before leaving office he had created fourteen forestry reserves, totaling more than 16 million acres.[18]

Conservationists had long been familiar with the border lakes and their special charms and began pushing for their protection, but on December 30, 1891, the Duluth Chamber of Commerce sent out petitions condemning the proposal. Had Pinchot or Fernow managed to create a forest reserve in northern Minnesota, the story of logging on the Winton watershed would have ended almost as it began, but public relations efforts by the industry persuaded many citizens to oppose the forest reserve plans. The *Ely Times* wrote in its December 4, 1891, issue, "The project to set aside 7,500,000 acres of some of the best mineral, timber and agricultural lands in the state as a National Park is universally denounced by all . . . as being an outlandish scheme, entirely devoid of sense or reason."

Despite reports of outrageous timber theft from school sections and areas fraudulently described as "swamps," public sympathy, especially in places like Winton, remained with the lumber companies. Ecological abuses escalated. Finally, it was widespread wildfire that compelled even the most pro-development booster to abandon pioneer notions and embrace conservation. Fire worked not only in the ecology of the landscape but also in the minds of the people, forcing decisions that have had almost as large an impact on the forests as fire itself. Fire accomplished what Pinchot and Fernow could not, motivating the public's opinion to the point that no senator dared argue against forestry, at least the fire suppression aspect of it. Fire was a primary shaper of the political discussion and had a fundamental influence on forest policy from the outset.

One prime example, the Hinckley, Minnesota, fire of September 1, 1894, was heinous, so large and hot it drew backdrafts up to eighty miles an hour, uprooting trees that exploded into flames. An eerie orange-green glow normally associated with tornadoes, typhoons, or hurricanes lit the skies while thick belts of smoke blanketed much of the land. A racing maelstrom of exploding gasses, the fire incinerated towns so quickly people simply could not get out of its way, much less fight it. Survivors reported a heat so intense that the wheels of railroad cars were welded to the tracks and nail kegs melted into a solid mass. One of those survivors, Peter Bilado, reported,

> It grew so dark about two o'clock that I thought a cyclone was coming, and we had to have the lamps lighted. We could see the reflection of the fire in the sky, and could hear a peculiar sound like thunder in the air. The fire came on us very suddenly. It seemed to come from above with a roaring sound something like a large body of falling water. Balls of fire seemed to be bursting in the air . . . the fire beat down, and it seemed as though the air was full of hot sand which fell like fine hail.

More than four hundred people burned to death that day.[19]

On September 21, 1894, the *Ely Times* reprinted a sensational *Chicago Tribune* story:

> The Minnesota state senatorial committee which has been investigating the thefts of pine timber . . . has found evidence that the terrible forest fires which recently swept the pine belt, extending

from that state into Wisconsin and Michigan, were started by
agents of the timber thieves. Scouts . . . have brought good
evidence to show that the agents of these predatory corporations
started forest fires . . . for the purpose of destroying all traces of
their depredations and making it impossible to determine . . . how
much timber had been cut. . . . These incendiary fires, it is said,
spread and were not extinguished 'till they had devastated a
thousand square miles of territory . . . Hinckley, Sandstone, and
a dozen or so other populous towns and resulted in the death of
many hundred[s] of people . . . it is not for the larceny of the pine,
but for manslaughter that every man . . . should be prosecuted.

In its final report, the committee provided not only physical evidence
of this crime but also the testimony of a man who claimed to have set
the Hinckley fire at the request of timber men who were trying to destroy telltale stumps.[20]

Public reaction to this fire bolstered proponents of forestry reform
and timber industry regulation, fear of another conflagration forcing
action where reason had not. In April 1895, the Minnesota legislature
named as chief fire warden conservationist Christopher C. Andrews,
who had read a paper, "The Prevention of Forest Fires," at the American Forestry Association meeting in Brooklyn, New York, just nine
days before the Hinckley catastrophe. Achieving the rank of major
general during the Civil War, Andrews had been appointed ambassa-
dor to Sweden and Norway in 1872 by President Ulysses S. Grant.
While there, Andrews studied European forestry and soon realized
that a rational land policy—a tree-planting program and fire suppression to preserve remaining pineries—would provide a real benefit to
Minnesota's forests. When Andrews returned from his overseas appointment, he pushed for the creation of a forestry school in the
United States and worked to raise public awareness of the calamity of
overharvest and the damage of wildfire.

When in 1900 Andrews petitioned Congress to create a forest reserve at Cass Lake, he was joined in his efforts by Pinchot and by
women's club delegates who traveled to Washington to testify their support. Finally, on June 27, 1902, Congress set aside 225,000 acres to be
managed by forestry principles, the first forest so designated in the
country. Andrews recalled:

It was a great triumph for forest conservation. On my first visit to Cass Lake [1898] the clean, beautiful forest extended to within a step or two of the shores. Imagine my surprise and indignation when on visiting the place [later] . . . I found the pine had been cut. It had been despoiled under the "dead and down" timber law.

The land eventually became part of the Chippewa National Forest. The Minnesota legislature also established the North Central Agricultural Experiment Station at the Minnesota College of Agriculture in Grand

*In logging's wake, with stacked slash as fuel and even-aged and combustible trees easily consumed by flames, forest fires often had devastating effects on the landscape.*

Rapids, and so began the state's first practical expression of forestry "on the ground."[21]

Despite progress in Minnesota, the national debate was far from over. On February 26, 1897, without warning, without consultation, lame-duck president Grover Cleveland acted on his inauguration promise and created thirteen more forestry reserves totaling 21,279,840 acres. He deliberately set aside twice as many as requested, noting, "A Republican will succeed me, and he will undo half of what I have done, so to be safe, I have done plenty." Outraged, western lumbering, mining, and grange organizations brought full pressure to bear on their congressional delegates. Six days later Wyoming senator Clarence D. Clark introduced an amendment to allow future presidents to erase Cleveland's pen stroke, the measure meeting with immediate approval.[22]

In the House, however, Iowa congressman John F. Lacey introduced a bill outlining tenets of the U.S. Forest Service that remain in place today. The bill authorized the Secretary of the Interior to open the reserves to use and to sell timber and minerals while instituting protective measures to prevent overuse or the destruction of associated watersheds. Lacey met with strong censure from western senators, who opposed conservation in any form. Pinchot wrote of this bitter struggle:

> Speaking in support of his amendment, Judge Lacey made a phrase which fitted the looting of the public lands as wallpaper fits the wall. Said he, "There is nothing so sacred as an abuse. There is nothing so adamant against change, nothing that excites such indignation when attacked, as a wrong way of doing things that people have got used to. Illegal privilege and maladministration entrenched in time are far harder to break through than the Maginot Line."[23]

President William McKinley had intimated that he would support the Senate and repeal Cleveland's forest reserves. But Charles Sargent, long-time activist and chairman of the National Academy of Sciences committee to investigate the condition of America's forests, interceded, telling the story to Henry S. Graves, who succeeded Pinchot as chief of the forest service:

> There was strong pressure on McKinley to annul Cleveland's action and our Commission called on him two days after his inauguration.

He was bent on returning Cleveland's reservation to the public domain and told us that he was going to do it. After our interview was over I went back alone and had a private interview with McKinley which lasted I think an hour. When it was over he had decided to let the reservation stand and take no action in the matter. I have always felt that this was the best day's work I ever put in for this country.

With this newfound ally, Pinchot formed a coalition and on June 4 passed the Forest Reserve Act of 1897, providing one hundred fifty thousand dollars to the Geological Survey to map the forest reserves and empowering the interior department to manage the land. Not long after this McKinley toured northern Minnesota, viewing the lands that would eventually become the Superior National Forest and the BWCAW.[24]

But the conservationists did not win the battle without casualties. Perhaps most damaging was a lieu-land clause, under which "the settler or owner" of a tract of land within a forest reserve could "select in lieu thereof a tract of vacant land" elsewhere on the public domain. Pinchot became aware of the ramifications of this provision only later, realizing that lumber, mining, or railroad companies could trade in worthless portions of their land grants—territory they had already stripped of resources—and choose instead the most valuable public domain land available.[25]

Worse, the Division of Forestry was still no more than a small office in the Department of Agriculture, with no jurisdiction over the forest reserves, those powers remaining with the impotent Department of the Interior. But Pinchot took every opportunity to educate timber men and the public, submitting canned articles to both the *Ely Miner* and the *Ely Times*. These articles discussed a variety of issues from fire protection to tree planting, exploring the benefits forests had on water and air quality and providing evidence that a strong forest service would benefit lumber interests directly and help support local economies. Finally, on July 1, 1900, Congress upgraded the division to a bureau and gave it a staff of 179. Pinchot's family endowed a Forestry Department at Yale which offered four-year degrees to train competent people for the new bureau.[26]

Then, through tragedy, the nation's wildlands gained an even more powerful supporter. On September 14, 1901, an anarchist killed President McKinley at the Pan-American Exhibition in Buffalo, New York, elevating Theodore Roosevelt to the presidency. Pinchot took his conservation idea to Roosevelt, who, he reported, "understood, accepted, and adopted it without the smallest hesitation." Indeed, in his first address to Congress Roosevelt stressed the importance of conservation:

> The character and uses of the remaining public lands differ wildly from those of the public lands which congress [had] especially in view when these laws were passed. The rapidly increasing rate of disposal of the public lands is not followed by a corresponding increase in home building.
>
> The attention of congress is especially drawn to the timber and stone law, the desert land law, and the commutation clause of the homestead law, which in their operation have in many respects conflicted with wise public land policy.[27]

An outdoorsman, rancher, and progressive, Roosevelt used his tenure as president to develop the themes of reform—of banking, labor, trade, and land policy. He exemplified a new attitude toward wildlands for those Americans who expected the public domain to supply recreation, rejuvenation, and peace of mind rather than wealth or opportunity. By 1904 Roosevelt had increased the forest reserves to 63 million acres.

*An avid outdoor recreationist, President Theodore Roosevelt adopted Pinchot's idea of conservation and created the national forest system.*

Abraham Lincoln—signer of the homestead law, rugged individual, railsplitter, self-educated farmstead child —embodied the spirit of the frontier he governed. In contrast, Roosevelt was an urbanite, a Harvard man, an asthmatic lawyer, a rotund New York politician. He learned to appreciate the value of wilderness when he fled the city in pain and grief over the near-simultaneous deaths of his wife and his mother. The stricken Roosevelt escaped to the wild North Dakota badlands to become a rancher, to live the "strenuous life" as he called it. Although he failed as a rancher and lost about half of his entire capital in the endeavor, Roosevelt learned to love western life, coming to understand and feel personally the spiritual and rejuvenating effects of untrammeled land on the modern psyche. His health and physique, as well as his attitude, improved in the wilds.

Pinchot accompanied Roosevelt on many of his expeditions. With great vigor, optimism, and aplomb, the two friends spread the message that science would preserve the nation's wildlands, that silvicultural techniques and forest fire suppression could create and maintain a timber supply ad infinitum without destroying the forest. The public relations policy begun twenty years earlier at the Columbian Exposition in Chicago was finally bearing fruit.

No previous president had taken such a firm pro-conservation position. Meanwhile, the lumbermen on the Winton watershed—Robert Whiteside, Bert and Martin Torinus, Herb Good, Arthur Swallow, and Louis Hopkins—were becoming increasingly open to Pinchot's message, with good reason. The difficulties lumbermen faced—huge expenditures on new mills and transportation routes, immense shipping bills to get their product to market, cutthroat business practices—were compounded by falling lumber prices. Despite the withdrawal of 63 million acres from the timber supply, despite the creation of industry organizations like the Mississippi Valley Lumberman's Association, formed in 1891, which worked to moderate production and foster cooperation, lumber prices tumbled.[28]

Industry universally failed at its attempts to stabilize the timber market, the incentives to overharvest being too strong. There was no motivation for lumbermen to preserve stands of timber, or even so-called seed trees, to replant or conserve in any way: timber left behind one year might be cut by a competitor, reserved by Pinchot and Andrews, or lost in a fire the next. Lumber companies glutted the markets with product and then cut even more as they tried to catch falling profits.[29]

As Pinchot's message of assured, sustained use of the forests, carefully regulated by the appropriate government body and supervised by Congress, made its way from Roosevelt's bully pulpit into the boardrooms of the timber companies, lumber barons began to see the usefulness of these notions. In Minnesota Christopher C. Andrews assured timber men, "The friends of forestry do not interfere with the cutting of timber. On the contrary, they wish the industry to be continuous."[30]

If control of the forests was turned over to the government and industry use of those forests insured, lumbermen would not have the expense of buying, protecting, and paying taxes on huge tracts of land. There would be no mad rush for timber or costs associated with fire suppression or rejuvenation of the cutover land. Andrews stated the cause of forestry most succinctly in his Fifth Annual Report to the Governor in 1899: "Forestry is the science of growing trees for profit." No lumberman would argue with that. And the biggest, most powerful lumber companies had already been given a full five years under the lieu-land clause to dispose of their worthless lands in the East and Upper Midwest and replace them with the best tracts of sugar pine in the South or redwood and douglas fir groves in the West. The lumber barons were ready for forestry.

In early January 1905, the Bureau of Forestry held the American Forest Congress to discuss the transfer of the forest reserves to the agriculture department and the creation of a forest service. The attendance list verifies Pinchot and Roosevelt's success in selling the notion of conservation to industry: F. E. Weyerhaeuser; Edward Hines; James J. Hill; Howard Elliot, president of the Northern Pacific Railroad; N. W. McLeod, president of the National Lumber Manufacturers Association; editors and publishers of industry trade magazines; representatives of the mining industry and cattlemen associations; the presidential cabinet; the Supreme Court; members of Congress; fifty-two governors of states, territories, and dependencies; seventy representatives of organizations, societies, and labor unions; and members of the Inland Waterways Commission.

Roosevelt addressed the assembly:

There is no other question now before the nation of equal gravity with the question of conservation of our natural resources, and it is the plain duty of us who, for the moment are responsible, to take inventory of the natural resources which have been handed to us, to forecast the needs of the future, and so handle the great resources of our prosperity as not to destroy in advance all hope of the prosperity of our descendants.[31]

All agreed that the status quo was far from ideal. Weyerhaeuser addressed the group, saying, "The next obstacle, more important because harder to overcome, is fire. I am frank enough to say that in this matter lumbermen themselves are largely responsible, sometimes even to the extent of fighting reform." Andrew Carnegie spoke on the conservation of ores and minerals, James J. Hill on the natural wealth of the land. Robert Alexander Long, president of the Long-Bell Lumber Company of Kansas City, Missouri, predicted that Lake States timber would be gone within a decade, southern yellow pine in twenty years, the Pacific Coast stands in only forty. Long pressed for governmental price supports for lumber and high tariffs on Canadian lumber.[32]

After this gathering, Congress passed HR 8460, which transferred the forestry reserves to the Department of Agriculture, created the Forest Service, repealed the much abused Timber and Stone Act, and modified the lieu-land clause. The Agricultural Appropriations Act of March 3, 1905, empowered forest service rangers to arrest lawbreakers on the reserves, to fight fire, and to sell timber and minerals, the proceeds to be used for further improvement of the reserves.

On the day of the transfer, Pinchot received from Secretary of the Interior James Wilson a letter which for Pinchot crystallized forestry's rationale: "In the administration of the forest reserves it must be clearly borne in mind that all land is to be devoted to its most productive use. . . . All the resources of forest reserves are for *use* . . . under such restrictions only as will insure the permanence of these resources." This earliest USFS memo clearly outlines the two guiding principles that directed the organization for almost a century: sustained yield and multiple use.[33]

Congress gave the president authority to set aside forestlands in 1891, the same year Ely incorporated as a city. On the Winton/Ely watershed would develop the last major logging boom to enjoy the pioneering freedom and wild ways of the past and the first to be restricted by the changing rules of conservation and progressive policies regarding labor. It was also the first place where new ideas about wilderness and then restoration would be implemented, changes in strategy guided by fire—first the fear of it, then the recognition of its utility.

# 7

## Foresters Under Fire

*As the moon rose higher the inessential houses began to melt away until gradually I became aware of the old island here that flowered once for Dutch Sailor's eyes—a fresh green breast of the new world. Its vanished trees, the trees that had made way for Gatsby's house, had once pandered in whispers to the last and greatest of all human drama; for a transitory enchanted moment man must have held his breath in the presence of this continent.*

F. SCOTT FITZGERALD, *The Great Gatsby*

---

MIDWAY THROUGH WINTON'S PEAK YEAR of production in the border lakes, on February 13, 1909, President Roosevelt established Superior National Forest, almost a million acres of rock, water, and tree scattered along the U.S.–Canada border, from Lake Superior in the east to Rainy Lake in the west. In contrast to the president's far-sighted gesture, public opinion toward forestry and the new national forest bordered on outright contempt. Locals feared federal foresters would lock away timber supplies, force the mills to close, and end mineral exploration and mining. Any governmental efforts to regulate the Swallow and Hopkins or St. Croix operations promised to be an uphill struggle.

An unlikely ally emerged to change local opinion: fire. One of two natural forces that had shaped the border lakes ecosystem—the other being ice, which had sculpted the landscape, removed the soil, and gouged out the myriad lakes—fire determined the species distribution

of both flora and fauna, established new, even-aged stands of trees after intermittent crown fires, and maintained older stands with periodic
ground fires. Before white settlement, tribal people had set repeated
fires in the pine belt to clear undergrowth, easing travel and facilitat-
ing hunting. Omer Stewart, one of the first researches to fully understand the extent to which aboriginals used fire to shape the landscape,
wrote in 1954:

> Minnesota has had some of the nation's most disastrous forest
> fires. One is the Hinckley fire of 1894, the other the Cloquet fire
> of 1918. These and the other excessively damaging fires, by the
> dates they occurred, lend weight to the belief that Indians kept
> forest open and free of underbrush by frequently setting fires that
> did not destroy the mature trees. When the Indians were removed
> from an area or were prohibited from continuing their ancient
> practices, brush accumulated so that fires, which inevitably came,
> were much more destructive than at the time of settlement. Min-
> nesota, being both a prairie and forest state, provides evidence
> that Indians burned fields and forests and that in both their fires
> were a decisive ecological factor.[1]

In the early years of Superior National Forest's existence, fire's
biggest impact was not on the region's ecology but on the local bias
against fledgling foresters. The change had begun earlier, after the
Hinckley disaster in 1894, when conservationist Christopher C. Andrews was appointed the state's forester.

Andrews had long understood the ecology of forests and fire. As
early as 1856 he wrote in the *Boston Post*, "Timber is a fundamental el-
ement of colonial growth. Minnesota has an abundance of excellent
timber. There is considerable stunted scrub oak also. The soil is not the
cause of their scrubby looks but the devouring fires which annually
sweep over the land." Even though he was an old man by the time he became state forester, Andrews did more to control the scourge of wildfire
in Minnesota's cutover pineries than any other individual.[2]

Still, the state's new forestry department lacked both authority and
funding. The legislature gave Andrews an annual budget of only five
thousand dollars to protect $100 million worth of timber. Arguing that
"forestry is not an expense, it is a savings account," Andrews requested

additional funds, but the legislature was slow to increase his budget. He estimated that St. Louis County alone still contained 1.5 million acres of forested land with 3.2 million feet of white pine and 700,000 feet of red pine. While none of this land was under Andrew's authority, all of it was under his protection.[3]

Like Pinchot and Fernow before him, Andrews used his appointment as a bully pulpit from which to preach the common sense of conservation. With such a limited budget, his best course of action was to educate the public on the benefits of forestry, ideally igniting a grassroots push for increased funding and inspiring the strong, local support that was needed to enforce laws on the public lands. His first year as fire warden, Andrews, armed with a stereopticon lantern, good notes, and one hundred slides, spoke to 349 groups about fire prevention and forestry. Earning the nickname "indefatigable Andrews," the distinguished old major general lectured anyone who would listen.

Also dependent on local support, Andrews's system of fighting forest fires involved selecting community leaders to be resident fire wardens. Andrews appointed C. P. Ireland and Thomas Lamb as wardens in Winton and gave the Ely post to John Densmore. The legislature gave wardens the power to arrest and fine violators or arsonists—anyone who caused wildfires, be they careless campers, farmers clearing their fields, or railroad companies whose engines spewed sparks along the right of way. Earning two dollars a day while performing their duties, wardens also could conscript men to help fight fires, these recruits earning one and a half dollars a day. Andrews issued circulars with instructions on fighting fires, planting trees, and building trails and roads. The system's benefits were clear: locals were

*As Minnesota's first chief fire warden, Christopher C. Andrews used his position to develop public awareness of fire's danger and to organize a system of local wardens to stamp out minor fires before they could become mighty conflagrations.*

closest to the fires and so in the best position to fight them, and no costs were incurred until there was a fire. After three years of recruitment and training, Andrews estimated that the wardens extinguished 61 percent of the state's forest fires.[4]

In 1898 there were only fifty-one fires in Minnesota, their combined damages under ten thousand dollars. By the eighth year of the warden system the destructive fires were limited to just thirty-four, causing $3,820 in damages. But this relative success bred complacency, and the legislature resisted implementing laws that would protect the state's forests from destructive logging practices or rehabilitate land already damaged by the clear cuts and firestorms of the past. The warden system was no replacement for a rational forest policy headed by an all-encompassing authority, what Pinchot had called conservation. The devastation of logging continued almost unabated in Minnesota, with both the public and the legislature ignoring pleas for more sweeping reform. A few bad fire years, however, inspired change.

In 1908 little rain fell, and fires soon raged across the continent. A January prairie fire in Harlem, New York, threatened the Consolidated Gas Company; later, more than five thousand men worked a fire line upstate. Desperate, the New York lumber companies hired Carl E. Myers, a self-proclaimed rainmaker, to launch a balloon designed to salt the clouds and cause rainstorms. While the fires in the East were widely reported, in the West they were far more damaging. A series of smoldering fires flared up in British Columbia and destroyed the coal mining towns of Fernie and Hosmer, killing more than seventy-five people.[5]

Despite Andrew's best efforts, Minnesota experienced its worst fire year since the Hinckley blaze of 1894. A series of fires, the largest of which was started by careless fishermen, joined together just east of Chisholm and swept over the community, destroying Weyerhaeuser's new paper mill. Most of the town's four thousand residents escaped to Hibbing by train; the rest took refuge in a lake. Andrews's wardens conscripted over five thousand men to battle the blazes, which eventually burned almost half a million acres. Insurance companies estimated the damage at over $1.5 million. Reawakened to fire's dangers, the public clamored for a solution, and in response the state legislature passed a new forest fire law in spring 1909. Among its measures, loggers were required to burn their slash before April of the following year, campfires were to have a ten-foot-wide circle cleared around them, and railroads were compelled to install spark arrestors on their engine smokestacks and clear fifty feet on each side of their tracks of any fuel.

While the fires of 1908 had motivated legislators, most people outside of Chisholm still accepted fire as a way of life, especially in rural communities where settlements met the wilderness. Locals believed the way to control fire was to remove the forests, allowing the blazes that inevitably followed logging to consume any remaining fuel, thereby leaving the land virtually fireproof. Many reasoned that the danger fire once posed in eastern forests had dissipated when the land was converted to farms. The fire warden in Becker County, Mr. Berg, reported his frustrations: "An active public sentiment cannot be awakened." Thomas Lamb of Ely wrote to Andrews of his own difficulties as fire warden: "Land owners take interest in forest preservation; others seem to be careless."[6]

Just months after the fires had stopped burning, apathy toward forestry practices was compounded by local suspicions over the federal government's intentions with the lands and resources of the newly created Superior National Forest. The *Ely Miner* ran its first piece on the subject in May 1909, an article that fanned local fears: "The government will take for forest preserve purposes all the land that lies within the limits that have been fixed. The Duluth land office has received no information as to how those in charge in Washington plan to deal with the holders of land in the forest reserve." The article speculated that privately held land within the boundaries of the new national forest, an area that included most of the timberlands belonging to Robert Whiteside, Swallow and Hopkins, Oliver Mining, and the St. Croix company, would simply be condemned and the owners paid a flat fee for their patents.[7]

The district forester in Missoula, Montana, responded to this paranoid misinformation with a letter that appeared on May 21:

> The creation of a National Forest does not in any way affect the patented land and valid claims which are included within its boundaries. Such lands will not be purchased by the government. . . .

Taken all in all, the Forest policy when thoroughly understood, ex-
emplifies the policy of the greatest good to the greatest number, and
its attitude toward forest users and the public in general is at
all times that of a square deal.

Judging by this example, the biggest challenge the new foresters
faced was in the realm of public relations. On May 1, 1909, when Scott
Leavitt arrived in Ely to take control as forest supervisor, he immediately set out to reassure the local community of forestry's benign intentions. Following Andrews's example, Leavitt traveled widely, addressing any organization that would have him, educating his listeners
and promoting forest conservation. But far, far more compelling than
his stereopticon slides and presentations were natural forces at work
on the border lakes.

Following on the heels of one drought-plagued year, the spring of
1909 was also dry. With little snow the previous winter, the forests
around Winton quickly dried to tinder. Soon they were burning. The
drought covered most of North America, the woes of Ely and Winton
shared by most of the communities adjacent to the new national
forests.

The drought continued into the next year. On June 17, 1910, the *Ely
Miner* published a front-page article by Christopher C. Andrews warning the public of the terrible fire danger: just a month into summer 189
fires had already burned over one hundred thousand acres in Minnesota. The *Ely Miner* wrote, "Forest fires have been raging in this vicinity for some time and have kept the forest rangers good and busy. A
crew of men left Wednesday morning to try to check the fires east of
Winton. Owing to the dry weather and the strong winds it is hard work
to accomplish any headway." A week later the paper reported large fires
in the Robinson Lake area, east of Fall Lake, in the Stony River country,
and north of town. Thick smoke enveloped both Ely and Winton, ob-
scuring the sun and requiring lamps to be lighted at midday.

On July 1, the *Ely Miner* ran the headline, "Much Fire Danger." The
woods were ablaze between Tower and Ely as the fire from the Robinson Lake area raced toward town. Other blazes encroached from the
south and west, and the wind picked up to thirty-five miles an hour,

raining cinders down on the settlement's wooden structures. Fire wardens Densmore, Lamb, and Ireland conscripted miners to dig a fire line along the town's outskirts while other crews raced about trying to extinguish the many spot fires caused by falling embers. For a while, they could barely keep pace with the flames, and it looked like the towns might be lost. With sundown, however, the wind slowed and the danger lessened.

Still there was no rain. Blazes flared up again, those in the Birch Lake area destroying a new school and burning out sixty families who were lucky to escape with their lives. Forest service crews struggled with a fierce fire near Everett Lake. Ely mayor Knutson closed all businesses, emptied the hotels and bordellos, and sent every able-bodied man out to the fire lines. The mayor further decreed it unlawful for anyone to fire a rifle, pistol, firework, squib, or blasting cap in the city until further notice and canceled all July 4 celebrations. The *Ely Miner* stated flatly, "The country needs a rain and needs it bad."[8]

Blazes raged across the border lakes, consuming whole townships between Sea Gull and Gunflint Lakes, in the cutover areas around Basswood Lake, near Trout Lake and Lake Vermilion, in the Robinson Lake and Eagles Nest Lake area, and from Ely south along the Stony River and Birch Lake all the way to the Laurentian Divide. The lumber and mining companies had crews trying to put out the fires; still, St. Croix lost two camps and many feet of logs in the Stony River area. Late that fall fires raged along the Canadian border near Rainy River. In October one blaze, known as the Baudette fire, consumed that town as well as Spooner, Graceton, and Pitt.[9]

The fires of 1910 forged unity, however, and once the crisis had passed many northern Minnesotans and citizens the nation over felt affection for the foresters, men who had worked so bravely and effectively, in some cases giving their lives, to protect rural towns. Though very destructive in terms of property and loss of life—over one million acres burned and more than $1.7 million in damages in Minnesota alone, forty deaths in the Baudette fire and almost eighty in the Pacific Northwest—the terrible fires of 1910 did much to galvanize support for the fledgling forest service. Public reaction to these fires dictated national fire policy for a century, as the suppression of forest fire took on patriotic overtones and became a cause that Americans rallied behind. Fire came to be viewed as an evil, to be exterminated at all costs.[10]

Joe A. Fitzwater assumed the post of forest supervisor in 1911. With public support behind him, he set about meeting his priorities, described in an *Ely Miner* article headlined "Excellent Work Being Done by the Forest Rangers":

> [Superior National Forest] has for its object, First—the protection of the present forest cover. Second—The cutting of merchantable timber in such a manner as to give an early second crop. Third— To stock by artificial means areas which will not reforest naturally. ... The first most important work on the Superior is keeping out of forest fires, since this is fundamental if anything is to be accomplished. .... As fast as appropriations allow, trails together with telephone lines, will be built through the more inaccessible districts.[11]

Acting almost immediately on that final promise, Fitzwater dispatched a six-man crew from Ely early that spring. They paddled White Iron Lake to Farm Lake, following the Kawishiwi to a high rock outcropping at a bend in the river where they built a fifty-foot lookout tower, attaching poles and a platform to a large standing pine tree. The

*The USFS's staff of foresters, including this 1925 crew, worked tirelessly to fight fires, plant trees, and rehabilitate the vast areas of cutover lands that became the national forests following tax forfeiture.*

tower became known as the Fernberg Lookout, a combination of two crewmembers' names, Ole Fernlund and John Handberg. The rangers cut a trail back to town and connected phone lines with the central office in Ely's Fenske Building. This trail, widened and improved over the years, eventually became the Fernberg Road.

Another ranger, C. A. Terry, built a station on the Echo River northwest of Ely. The pathway to this station was later widened and extended into the Echo Trail. Leavitt built a third ranger station, the Baird Station, four miles north of the St. Croix Headquarters Camp on the Stony Tote Road. Each station consisted of a five-room log cabin, a stable large enough for four horses, a pasture, and a kitchen garden. By the end of the summer the Kawishiwi District had over twenty-seven miles of telephone line strung throughout the forest, connecting the lookout towers, the stations, and the office in Ely.[12]

In 1912, the forest service installed phone lines from Ely to Harding by extending the St. Croix line south from Everett Lake to DeCaigney's Lake Portage. Rangers strung another line from Bald Eagle Lake to Lutsen via Baird Ranger Station on the Stony River. With the forest from Grand Marais to International Falls connected by phone lines, a fire spotted anywhere could be reported immediately rather than days or even a week later, after the ranger had paddled or hiked back to the USFS office in Ely.

Even with this technological innovation, one of the main obstacles to fighting fire in northern Minnesota remained: an almost complete lack of roads. Because the skid trails and ice roads used by loggers in the winter were mostly impassable in the summer, the only way early forest rangers could travel north during the warmer months was by canoe or via Herb Good's two railroad lines. As Supervisor Leavitt reported, "There were no highways into the Superior region in 1909. Except for a few short stretches between local points, there were no roads at all." The longest roads were the Stony Tote Road and the Whitesides' old county wagon road from Tower to Ely. There was a road from Winton to Ely, but the connection from Ely to Burntside Lake, begun in 1899, was not complete until 1914. Other thoroughfares in the area were poorly developed or treacherous during summer's fire season. Men and equipment traveled over the logging railroads or game trails or via canoes to reach the fires. Often it was days before a crew could get to a blaze, and by then the fire might be raging out of control. Increasingly, road building became a duty of the forest service, but, as the lumber companies well knew, it was expensive and slow work in the rough country of the Superior National Forest.[13]

Finally, in 1916, a federal program called "The Good Roads Bill" provided $1 million for ten years apportioned to counties within the national forests, followed up in 1918 with a second appropriation of $9 million and in 1921 with a third of $15 million. Old Highway 1, the Stony Tote Road, was extended to Finland and Beaver Bay by 1922. The Lake Superior tract was improved and open to automobile traffic from Duluth to Grand Marais. The branch to Ely remained Highway 1; the lakeshore branch became Highway 61. The Gunflint Trail by 1918 snaked from Grand Marais north to Sea Gull Lake and Highway 1.

Supervisor Fitzwater also began a reforestation program late in the summer of 1911. As the white pine cones matured, rangers gathered about twenty-five bushels of seed. Earlier in the season, rangers had prepared a nursery, the Birch Lake plantation near the Baird Ranger Station, an area that had been logged over and burned in the 1910 fires. In 1914 rangers gathered 40,000 pounds of white pine seed, replanted 30,000 acres of the forest, and planted 175,000 pine near Clark Lake. The following year, in cooperation with the national forest, the Minnesota State Forestry Board planted 750,000 trees in northern Minnesota. Les Brownell, a local ranger, planted 50,000 pine seedlings in the Birch Lake area that spring. Meanwhile, the state forester, together with rangers from the Superior, put 160,000 Norway and 40,000 white pine seedlings on Burntside State Forest. Later that year, the State Forestry Board purchased another 800,000 seedlings from commercial nurseries to plant in northern Minnesota.[14]

Dedicated to his many-pronged forestry plan, Fitzwater in his first year also held a timber sale, the 735-acre Birch Lake Sale, which went to St. Croix Lumber. In 1913 and 1914 the company bought 2,440 acres for $3,442.43, and in 1915 another thousand acres of white pine stumpage for $9,236.85. Edward Hines Lumber bought 180 acres for $1,333.75. Swallow and Hopkins's first timber purchase from the Superior came in 1915 when it paid $4,689.11 for 2,320 acres of scattered white, red, and jack pine. In 1918 Herb Good bought the timber off 20,000 acres of forestland for $91,250. The widely fluctuating per-acre price represents the difference in species the tracts contained, with the remaining white and red pine commanding higher prices and jack pine and pulpwood selling for far less. In its first two decades, Superior National Forest had fifty-four timber sales, covering 32,160 acres that contained 44.6 million board feet, raising $130,662 in proceeds for national forest coffers.[15]

Even these well-planned sales were subject to abuse and fraud, however. Although the foresters carefully marked sale boundaries, many loggers persisted in the practice of cutting so-called section 37 or round or rubber forties, all euphemisms for clearing any timber they could reach that season, within the sale's limits or not. In addition, while the foresters carefully marked seed trees—usually the largest and healthiest in the area—to reserve them from the sales, logging companies often cut those coveted trees first. Once the seed trees were down, there was no way to prove they had ever been there, making prosecution, not to mention natural regeneration, difficult.

This evidence aside, the foresters and the Winton lumbermen managed to forge a tentative truce, an uneasy alliance. Despite the authority the federal government had invested in the new foresters to sell trees and to protect watersheds, they wielded their power lightly, knowing that any progressive forest management would be impossible without at least tacit industry support and cooperation. As late as 1922, lumbermen still owned more than a third of the land within Superior National Forest.[16]

A new industry was also drawing the foresters' attention: tourism. In 1900 there were only 4,200 automobiles in the entire nation; by 1915, almost a million. When World War I prevented people from traveling abroad, many decided to see America by car, selecting the newly created national forests as favored destinations. Superior National Forest's accessibility to tourists grew as roads were built for the logging companies. Whereas in the early days logs could be floated to the mills in Winton, by the 1920s loggers were cutting pulp trees—which do not float well—almost exclusively. Pulp logs were hauled on trucks, driven over new roads winding through the forest. As the pace of St. Croix and Swallow and

Hopkins's logging slowed, these roads and the tourists who used them became an increasingly important resource for the foresters to manage.[17]

But the foresters' training was in silviculture, the science of harvesting trees, not in recreation. Forestry is not preservation of untrammeled lands—what tourists were interested in seeing—but is rather, as Gifford Pinchot called it, "the art of the second growth," or, more simply put, tree farming. The service had been established to provide trees to avert a timber famine and to support local economies, economies based on timber production. With this myopic focus, the USFS used the ancillary activities of fire suppression, road building, and even tree planting as required to meet industry demands, tending to ignore recreation, even wildlife biology, altogether.

As early as 1913 the Superior National Forest and the Ely Chamber of Commerce began a joint venture to boost recreational opportunities in the northland. A booklet titled "Playground of a Nation" advertised amenities, including a map of summer resorts and camping, canoeing, hunting, and fishing opportunities. People from Chicago, Milwaukee, Green Bay, Detroit, Kansas City, and other midwestern towns streamed to the Superior, quickly making it one of the most visited national forests in the country. These tourists came north to escape the industrial, not to commune with it, and many were shocked to find clear cuts along the roads in their national forest. Groups formed to voice anti-logging sentiment and to push for greater protection of the wilderness.

The Minnesota Conservation Federation reported in 1943: "Not only is outdoor recreation a distinct social benefit but it is also important economically. . . . By 1932 it represented a private investment of $20,500,000 and gave employment to 13,000 people." In 1925, 14,968 people visited the Superior for recreation, each staying an average of four and one-half days. Ranger F. P. Leggett wrote:

> It is hardly possible to give recreational resources a valuation but some recreation engineers have insisted on doing it and have figured recreation as worth ten cents an hour or one dollar per day. Taking these figures for what you consider them worth, the Forest then provided $67,356.00 worth of recreation last year. Capitalized at four per cent the resource was worth then $1,683,900.00 last year.

That same year, Superior National Forest raised about $5,273.85 from its stumpage sales. Despite the northern foresters' indifference to tourism, that industry has always generated more income there than logging. The cutover and burnt Superior, plagued with expensive transportation problems due to the weather, the rugged terrain, and the lakes, had a hard time making any money from its trees, its century-old pine earning no more than a few pennies each. To make the forest pay, Minnesota foresters had to learn to manage recreation resources earlier than their colleagues. They had to shift their focus, moving from a land management paradigm based on resource extraction, Pinchot's conservation model, to a wholly new strategy.[18]

In the first official recognition of recreation as a legitimate use of the national forest, Congress on March 4, 1915, permitted the forest service to lease small tracts for summer homes and resorts and for other general recreational purposes. The USFS chose two places for this new program—Minnesota's border lakes and Colorado's Trappers Lake—and hired young landscape architect Arthur Carhart to plat cabin sites it would lease. At his first assignment, Trappers Lake, Carhart set about surveying roadways and mapping other important infrastructure along the beautiful shores of the high elevation glacial mere. The old cowhands who made up the rangers force in those days ironically dubbed the bright young man the "Beauty Doctor."[19]

Carhart soon understood why the old-timers derided him, for the great visual appeal of Trappers Lake slowly overcame him as he worked. He began to view the project in a different light, wondering whether the tasteful drifts of bright little cottages he was planning were merely more clutter, the meandering road encircling the jewel-blue lake nothing more than a cement necklace. Carhart worried that he was ruining the peace and majesty of the place, but he met his obligations. Later that summer he left for phase two of his assignment, in Minnesota's border lakes.

As Carhart paddled the Superior plotting cabin sites, tourist complexes, and access roads, the vague uneasiness of his Colorado experience coalesced into a policy recommendation, a bold move for such a young man. Carhart's reaction to the landscape was spiritual, an idea springing from the land itself and from the effect of rock, water, and

tree on his psyche and on his soul. For the first time he saw clearly that
the works of man could not improve some places. This was the genesis
of a new land ethic as profound as Pinchot's early notions about conservation: the wilderness idea.

When Carhart returned, refreshed and inspired, from the border
lakes, he told Regional Forest Supervisor Carl Stahl, "Unless we save
some places like this where people can really escape to the fullest the
grind of routine living, we're just not going to have any such outdoor
sanctuaries left." Stahl held up the cabin plan while he thought over
Carhart's ideas. Years later, the boldness of his report still astonished
Carhart, who wrote, "I had merely soaked up a truth, and it had found
its way into the typed pages."[20]

On December 6, 1919, at the regional offices in Denver, Carhart met
wildlife biologist Aldo Leopold. A decade earlier, Leopold had signed
on with the forest service and gone to New Mexico Territory, where he
quickly became concerned about diminishing game supplies. From the
unique perspective of a hunter and a wildlife biologist, he saw trends
that had been hidden to the timber producers. Leopold wrote articles
and published a newsletter about wildlife preservation, recommend-
ing that areas of the southwest's Gila Mountains be set aside as wilderness in order to protect game. His training gave him a broader view
than the landscape architect's: Carhart thought in terms of vistas while
Leopold considered habitats. Realizing that protecting a few lakes or
high elevation cirques would not safeguard a wilderness, Leopold expanded Carhart's wilderness idea.

In a 1921 *Journal of Forestry* article, Leopold defined wilderness as "a
continuous stretch of country preserved in its natural state, open to
lawful hunting and fishing, big enough to absorb a two weeks' pack trip,
and kept devoid of roads, artificial trails, cottages, or other works of
man." Leopold was not the sole promoter of this idea. His thoughts
were echoed by Carhart that same year in an article published by the
*Ely Miner*:

> Ely is destined to be one of the greatest outfitting points for trips
> into vacation land. It is very probable that in years to come
> the mere mention of a canoe will make the hearer think of Ely,

Minnesota, or the mention of Ely will call to the mind a wonder-
land of lakes and streams where the canoeist will find his ideal
territory.

The usual idea of the average person when thinking of developing a recreation territory is that there should be great hotels and
fine auto roads. Nothing could be more removed from the actual
situation in the Superior. While there must be certain highways
and certain hotels to bring people to the edge of the canoe country
and keep them while they are outfitting, the whole development
should be boat or canoe travel exclusively.[21]

The Superior National Forest supervisor at the time, Calvin A.
Dahlgren, was a cowboy from Idaho who did not swim and was more
comfortable on a horse than in a canoe. At first he clung to the ambi-

*At this 1930s tourist camp on Shagawa Lake, visitors take pleasure in the captivating
vistas and recreational opportunities the Ely region afforded.*

tious road-building plans he had envisioned for Superior, but in the end Carhart won him over to the wilderness idea. In the June 1921 edition of *Fins, Feather, and Fur,* the official bulletin of the Minnesota Game and Fish Department, Dahlgren wrote of the logical conclusion he had reached: "Every part of the forest is accessible by water, and should roads be built only a small part would be reached by them. The eastern part of the forest, less accessible than the western, will be devoted to canoe travel."[22]

Local sentiment reaffirmed Carhart and Dahlgren's vision. On April 23, road-building opponents held a public hearing in Duluth, those in attendance evidencing the broad support the wilderness idea enjoyed: Carl Stahl, Denver's assistant district forester and Dahlgren's boss; Thomas Whitten, the former St. Croix company manager, now employed by the Virginia and Rainy Lake Company; T. H. Little, St. Louis county commissioner; R. W. Acton, St. Louis County highway engineer; Donald Hough, *St. Paul Daily News* reporter; C. N. Hillman, *Two Harbors Chronicle* editor; H. B. Fryberger, on behalf of International Timber Company; Theodore Wirth, American Institute of Park Executives and American Park Society president; Herman T. Olson, representing Tower's Commercial Club; James A. Lawrie, on behalf of the Boy Scouts of America; C. B. Hoel, representing the Gilbert, Minnesota, Commercial Club; Rodney Paine, Jay Cooke State Park superintendent; Will H. Dilg, Izaak Walton League of America president; and H. J. Merdink, on behalf of Ely's Commercial Club. This distinguished group passed the following measure:

Be it resolved that recommendations be made to the Federal Government that the Federal Government acquire by purchase all the land between the two Forest segments [what is now the Echo Trail corridor], from the Forest north to the International Boundary.

Be it further resolved that it be recommended to the Secretary of Agriculture that the road building program be postponed at least one year so that a more thorough study can be taken.

Be it resolved to recommend to the Secretary of Agriculture and the United States Forest Service that a more thorough study be made of the Superior National Forest, which will take into account every possible feature of development, economic, recreational, scenic and aesthetic, with a view that its final development will give the highest possible service to all the people of the United States.[23]

Preserving the border lakes as wilderness has always had strong local support. To promote wilderness recreation, Stahl created a special administrative parcel within the Superior Forest, a "roadless area," a district in his opinion better suited to canoe recreation than to car camping, where no access roads would be built. Temporary logging roads, so-called winter roads, were not at odds with the "roadless" designation in Stahl's mind, so long as they did not interfere with recreation.

The qualification was largely moot at the time, as timber men were leaving the region. Forest service efforts to stabilize the local timber industry had failed. Stumpage prices were so low that the forests, especially remote ones, were almost valueless. The long-term return on managing cleared, burnt land for a second growth of trees was far less, not to mention more uncertain, than other investments. Lumber companies could not afford the extended capital forestry required, especially since there was no guarantee that fire, windstorm, or pest would not consume many decades of investment in a single season.

All of these obstacles might have been overcome and industry enticed to practice forestry on their lands, but excessively high property taxes tipped the balance sheet against these efforts. As early as 1907, Andrews had promoted reduced taxes on lands managed for forestry, but his recommendations initially went unheeded. While an Arbor Day law passed in 1871 paid a bounty for trees planted on the prairies, tree planting in the pine belt received no such support. Finally, in 1927, amidst a flurry of forest legislation, Minnesota passed the Auxiliary Forest Tax Law, allowing private owners to apply to have their cutover lands reclassified as "auxiliary forests" until they grew back. If the State Forestry Commission and the local county board of commissioners approved the application, the state reduced the property tax to a flat eleven cents an acre for fifty years, renewable once for another fifty years. Any timber cut from the land was taxed at ten percent of its value.[24]

Weyerhaeuser's Cloquet Lumber and Northern Lumber Companies applied for reclassification of 172,000 acres of cutover lands in St. Louis

County, much of it within the boundaries of Superior National Forest. The State Forestry Board was enthusiastic about the application, but the county commissioners rejected it, claiming the resulting loss of revenue would severely limit funds needed for county services. At the time, Weyerhaeuser was paying up to sixteen cents per acre in property taxes, plus eleven cents per acre for fire protection. The practical lumberman abandoned the land, along with a $1.25 million expansion of his Cloquet mill. Weyerhaeuser gave up another 68,656 acres in 1937 and later forfeited additional lands. Like other loggers, he was looking toward the West Coast. While the Weyerhaeuser Timber Company held nearly two million acres of timberland in the Pacific Northwest by 1914, it was only in the 1920s, after pulling out of the Midwest, that the company began to produce timber and other forest products with any vigor there. Despite the forest service's best efforts, the next stage in the industry's long history of migration had begun.[25]

# 8

## Defining a Wilderness

*To see the world in a grain of sand,*
*And a Heaven in a wild flower,*
*Hold infinity in the palm of your hand*
*And eternity in an hour.*
*A robin redbreast in a cage*
*Puts all Heaven in a rage.*
*A dove house fill'd with doves and pigeons*
*Shudders Hell thro' all its regions*
*A dog starved at his master's gate*
*Predicts the ruin of the state*

    WILLIAM BLAKE, "Auguries of Innocence"

---

AFTER THE LUMBER COMPANIES abandoned the border lakes in the 1920s, tax rolls collapsed. Denied the revenue and jobs logging had brought, Winton felt the pain of recession years before Black Monday spelled out the impending bust to the rest of the nation. Despite a nearly 1,209 percent increase in the pulp and wood-fiber harvest—from 22,000 cords in 1904 to 266,000 in 1929—total lumber production in Minnesota had slipped to just 2.6 percent of its peak year, 1899. The number of mill workers and loggers tumbled from 23,856—25 percent of the state's workforce—in 1909 to 4,000 by 1930. Profits for the companies remained high, but the pulpwood industry did not succor local communities as the pine boom had. This truth had been noted much earlier by the *Ely Miner*: "Timber once formed a large part of the natural wealth of this section, but as far as Ely and its immediate vicinity is concerned, that has been exhausted years ago. . . . In the city of Ely, there is little value in the way of real estate or personal property."[1]

The start of the downward spiral was 1907. Relentless in northern Minnesota, the depression began two decades earlier than in other areas of the country, the forests exhausted, the mills closed. In the late 1920s, when resources totally disintegrated, dark days visited the northland. The pioneer lumbermen and lumber barons, the boomers who had applauded progress, who were responsible for the devastation of the forests, were not around to see the end result of their work.

Billy Winton, the town's namesake, died on March 14, 1912, in Los Angeles, California, of typhoid pneumonia. Frederick Weyerhaeuser followed him two years later, his death acknowledged in Winton with the mills and city offices closed and flags at half-mast. Seeking the increasingly elusive frontier, one of the Torinus brothers moved to Montana and became a wheat farmer, but again he went bust, dying penniless. George C. Swallow died on August 2, 1917, in Milwaukee, Wisconsin, leaving an estate worth $67,512.25, one-half of Swallow and Hopkins's net worth, to his son, Arthur C. Swallow. The mill struggled for a short time more, but finally the band saws stopped rolling. On March 11, 1921, Louis J. Hopkins, then living in the Chicago suburb of Winnetka, and Arthur C. Swallow sold the mill and timber leftovers to Weyerhaeuser's Cloquet and Northern Lumber Companies for one dollar and "other valuable considerations." In its twenty years of existence, Swallow and Hopkins had taken about a billion board feet of pine from the border lakes.[2]

In 1925, thirty-three years after Robert Whiteside and Sam Knox opened the mill on Fall Lake, the St. Croix Lumber and Manufacturing Company officially sold its operations, the decision described in the company's minutes:

A special meeting of the Board of Directors of the St. Croix Lumber & Manufacturing Company was held. . . . Mr. Mortimer Hudson, the secretary, stated that proposals had been received from Joseph

Goodman and Sam Ager of Chicago to purchase the Company's
Real Estate, Buildings and Personal Property located at the Town of
Winton, Minnesota. The timber had long since been cut, the mill
had been dismantled and the Real Estate, Buildings and what
Personal Property was there would not again be needed by the
Company and that the sale of the property to them at the price
offered was desirable.[3]

The first to arrive was the last to depart. Frank Swan, Robert Whiteside's secretary, wrote in the office calendar for Sunday, September 19,
1931: "Mr. Whiteside passed away at 2:00 A.M. bringing to a close the
life of a noble gentleman with a character of sterling excellence whose
happiness was in helping others, the whole record of his life was that of
unselfish generosity." With this lofty praise, the era of pioneer logging
on the Winton watershed had reached its end.[4]

The year Whiteside died, 48 percent of the taxable land on the Arrowhead—6,830,840 acres—was tax delinquent. Winton's population,
nearly five hundred in 1909, had withered to just one hundred souls. In
1939 the National Resources Committee declared northern Minnesota
"one of the Nation's most critical social and economic problems." The
average annual income in the northland was a scant $453.40. In St.
Louis County 215 families, 500 people, lived on less than three hundred
dollars per family per year. Even this pitiful sum was artificially high,
for 32 percent of the total, ninety-three dollars on average, came from
depression-era public works jobs, employment with road crews or forest fire gangs.[5]

In 1934 Governor Floyd B. Olson established a committee on land
utilization to assess northern Minnesota and recommend a use for
what Olson described as "millions of acres of non-taxpaying, virtually
waste land, which originally included some of the most valuable land
in the state." The committee found that taxes were paid on less than
half of the state's forestland. On 16,634 square miles in northern Minnesota, an area larger than Massachusetts, Rhode Island, and Con-
necticut combined—70 percent or more of the land was in arrears. In
1934, St. Louis County's tax delinquency was, incredibly, nearly $4 mil-
lion. Governor Olson wrote:

Minnesota thus finds itself face to face with a new public domain. This new public domain is no longer a rich timbered land, such as once was . . . but land largely stripped of its natural wealth, for the most burned over and of low value.

The solution of the land problem of our state is by far the biggest conservation problem today, because it underlies all other phases of conservation.[6]

Only 40 percent of the land within Superior National Forest's boundaries was publicly owned in the 1920s, but in the 1930s and 1940s, as timber men abandoned their cutover property for taxes, locals who had once decried the locking away of land begged first the state and then the federal government to purchase the lands. The na-

*At the turn of the twentieth century, northern Minnesota was a "wasteland" of glacial rock and charred stumps left in the wake of industrial logging.*

tional forest picked up 60 percent of once privately held lands in arrears within its boundary, and the federal government declared four new state forests and added a million acres to the Superior. The land was cut over, its second growth cleared and its seed stock burnt—a white elephant under the forest service's care. The USFS paid no state or county taxes but promised the county 25 percent of its meager receipts—money raised through the timber sale program and fees from special use permits for cabins, resorts, quarries, grazing, and hydroelectric dams located on USFS lands. Ten percent of its revenues went to road building and maintenance, the rest to support the service itself (see table, below).[7]

Superior National Forest's revenues were pitifully small: not even lumbering wizard Frederick Weyerhaeuser could have turned a profit in those early years. However, the Superior was home to one remaining jewel, land where virgin forests still contained stands of jack pine and spruce with scattered pockets of large, old white and red pine: Carl Stahl's roadless area. In 1902, Christopher C. Andrews had convinced the Government Land Office to withdraw from sale much of the area. The rugged land's natural barriers protected its trees during the pine boom, and they remained unexploited in the 1920s.

In 1929, the USFS issued Regulation L-20, giving the chief forester, at the time R. Stewart, the power to establish "Primitive Areas" in the national forests. Stewart made the core of Stahl's roadless region the

| Superior National Forest Receipts, 1933–41 | | |
|---|---|---|
| | 25 PERCENT | 10 PERCENT |
| 1933 | $ 375.22 | $ 150.00 |
| 1934 | $ 365.24 | $ 146.00 |
| 1935 | $ 461.90 | $ 184.76 |
| 1936 | $ 1,119.97 | $ 447.99 |
| 1937 | $ 3,846.49 | $1,538.60 |
| 1938 | $ 2,951.55 | $1,180.62 |
| 1939 | $ 3,352.97 | $1,344.19 |
| 1940 | $ 6,647.84 | $2,659.14 |
| 1941 | $10,213.97 | $4,085.59 |

Source: Minnesota Conservation Federation, *Factual Information Concerning Minnesota's National Forests*, Hopkins, MN: The Federation, 1943.

Boundary Waters Canoe Area, also establishing the Flat Tops Primitive Area in Colorado and Leopold's Gila Primitive Area in New Mexico. In these areas, according to L-20, there would be "no roads or other provision for motorized transport, no commercial timber cutting, and no occupancy under special use permit for hotels, stores, resorts, summer homes, organization camps, hunting and fishing lodges, or similar uses." The BWCA was the largest area of virgin wilderness in the eastern United States. Only one-fourth of it had been logged when the depression began.[8]

During the desolate decades of the 1920s and 1930s, timber planners forgot the BWCA and the roadless area surrounding it. Without roads, there was no way to move the timber out. Logging was limited to small family outfits—like those run by Cy Fortier, Harry Homer, Jacob Pete, and the Kainz brothers—that contracted with the large paper mills in Cloquet, Duluth, and International Falls or ran small portable sawmills, cutting for the mines and other local retail outlets. Beginning in the 1930s, however, with the help of Civilian Conservation Corps labor, the USFS laid the infrastructure necessary to overcome the roadless area's natural defenses and began to offer large pulpwood and pine sales there. Advances in transportation had made it affordable to haul these remnant tracts of virgin landscape to the mill.

Trucks revolutionized the lumber industry, for with motorized vehicles and other heavy equipment a few men could do the work of dozens. One chainsaw replaced crews of sawyers; one man in a bulldozer replaced swampers, plows, groove cutters, ice wagons, road monkeys, and teamsters. Trucks, dozers, and feller bunchers finally conquered the ruggedness of the border lakes. Technology provided the means and World War II the markets. Vast forests fell to fuel the war: 50 million board feet a year went to make gunstocks alone. Superior sold 9.1 million board feet in 1940, but the harvest jumped to 45 million board feet by 1945 and to more than 97 million by 1952. At the war's end, wood prices had doubled.[9]

The harvest inside the roadless area began in 1939 when the firm Carlson and Oppel cut just west of Angleworm Lake, hauling the timber over a winter road down Spring Creek Draw southwest for three miles to the Echo Trail and then to the Northwest Paper Company in

Cloquet. In the 1940s Jacob Pete, son of one of the area's original pioneer loggers, used the old Cloquet Line as a roadbed and began logging east of Angleworm and north to Home Lake. Pete put a portable sawmill on Angleworm Lake, repaired the defunct bridges, and hauled in gravel to fill the grade of the old Swallow and Hopkins railroad line, using trucks to supply the mill year-round. In 1941 another local man, Harry Homer, began logging the Cummings Lake area south of Big Moose Lake and the Echo Trail and west of the north arm of Burntside Lake. Oliver Mining Company owned most of the timber, and the wood went to its mines in Ely and Tower. In 1944 North Star Logging Company cut pulp off the Davis Lake area west of Winchell Lake and north of Brule Lake. In this gyppo operation, the loggers were paid for each eight-foot pulp stick they cut, and trucks hauled the logs out of the roadless area over winter roads to Two Harbors, where the wood was shipped to pulp mills in Michigan.[10]

Winter roads were rough affairs. Usually in December, after the ground had frozen, lumbermen cleared any stumps, forest litter, or rocks from the path with a bulldozer. Stripped of snow and other insulation, the right of way froze even more solid, and, once the ground had a week to firm up, even heavily loaded logging trucks could traverse bogs, fens, and shallow streams for a few months each year. Then, in 1946, the USFS began construction of a permanent access road into the roadless area, twenty-six miles east from the old Stony Tote Road: Forest Road 173, the Tomahawk Road, twisting through the bogs of the Hundred Mile Swamp to Lake Isabella. Its namesake, the Tomahawk Timber Sale, was the largest transaction within the roadless area, nearly 130 square miles or 155,000 acres stretching north, east, and west of Lake Isabella. Cuts from this sale would continue for twenty years, justifying the expense of building an improved, permanent roadway.

During the Tomahawk cut's first years, gyppos lived in small wagons set up in a muddy forest clearing. Many brought their families to the bleak wilderness, and the small shantytown became temporarily urban, with a schoolhouse, recreation center, restaurant, sawmill, barracks, mess hall, even a post office, known as Forest Center, on site. The Duluth, Missabe and Iron Range Railroad built an extension from the main line to this camp, from which Tomahawk shipped pulp logs directly to its Kraft Paper mills in Wisconsin, along with pine crating, pallet lumber, and other rough-sawn products made at the mill in Forest Center. The gyppos hauled logs from the woods to the railhead with trucks, traveling on winter roads that spread like spider webs into the roadless area and lands south, Forest Center being the network's hub. In all, Tomahawk took 1.7 billion board feet of pulpwood, an amount almost equal to what Swallow and Hopkins and St. Croix Lumber had taken from the border lakes.[11]

By 1960 Superior National Forest had sold almost all of the federal timber in the southeastern portion of the roadless area. A decade earlier, Northland Paper Company bought a fifteen-square-mile block of stumpage. In 1954 Consolidated Paper, another Wisconsin firm, went into competition with Tomahawk, buying thirty-eight square miles of mixed jack pine, black and white spruce, white and red pine, white cedar, balsam fir, aspen, and birch, the Finn Lake Sale. With the Blandin Sale in 1956, winter roads began spreading into the rugged lands northwest of Ely. Twenty-five miles up the Echo Trail loggers cut trees in the Nina Moose Lake and Ramshead Lake area and west of the Moose River.

With these numerous sales and improvements, the roadless area was no longer roadless. The "temporary" roads included bridges, graveled roadbeds, and culverts, and, while most visitors were unaware of industry's presence in the wilderness, the area's growing popularity for both recreation and logging increased the potential for conflict. Visitors complained of the noisy trucks and chainsaws and the desolate clear cuts. But even though the BWCA was the most visited wilderness area in the nation, making recreation the obvious top priority, foresters remained steadfast to their original mission: timber production. Then, in 1958 the number of roads in violation of Stahl's original decree forced a change, as activists argued that the graveled labyrinth mocked the wilderness idea. They demanded an end to logging within the roadless area; in opposition, the Superior, which had very little legislative oversight or mandates, scrapped the roadless designation altogether.

Once the Superior had removed this obstacle, the service became more aggressive in its timber sale program, offering in 1960 the West Tofte block, an eighty-square-mile sale, the following year the East

Tofte block, twenty-two square miles, and in 1963 the Bellow Creek Area. These parcels were cleared with the new practices of highly mechanized pulpwood logging. Continued technological advances resulted in large, rubber-tired, four-wheel-drive skidders, feller bunchers, and steel-tracked bulldozers that did much greater ecological damage than had the early pine lumbermen with their Percherons and Morgans. These machines could operate year-round, even when the ground was not frozen and soils and new growth were unprotected by snow. While in the old days jacks had stacked the slash by hand, now bulldozers scraped the slash and stumps into huge piles for burning, destroying most of the young growth on the site in the process. Wilderness advocates argued that the forest was vanishing beneath the clattering steel tracks of heavy machinery.[12]

Even so, recreational use of the national forest continued to grow. By 1960 the need for wilderness foreseen by Carhart and Andrews had become more than spiritual or philosophic. Recreation was a major industry in Ely and Winton, both the demand and the dollars climbing steadily each year.

As early as 1916 the *Ely Miner* had proclaimed: "Tourists are arriving on every train and by auto from all over the country and are enjoying the canoe trips, the camping on the lakes and Burntside facilities to the utmost. 'The Playground of a Nation' maps issued by the Commercial Club are being sought, and from all parts of the globe requests for them are coming in."[13]

In 1917 seventeen thousand people visited the Superior; in 1945, about one hundred thousand. By 1965 almost two million, with many coming specifically to paddle the wilderness. In 1959 more than sixty thousand people spent an average of five days in the roadless area—three hundred thousand visitor days. From 1966 to 1969, the BWCAW was the nation's most visited forest area. In 1975 the Superior recorded 2.5 million visitor days, in 1985, 2.9 million, and by 1993, 3.9 million.[14]

Arthur Carhart's prediction had come to pass: Ely was synonymous with canoeing. The loons' lonely call, the game and fish, the crisp star-filled nights, the still water reflecting gossamer aurora borealis—these sensory experiences had real economic value to city or plains dwellers. One wry wilderness advocate, Ernest Oberholtzer, predicted, "When you destroy the beauty of that region, you destroy its utility." Superior National Forest's industrial logging program threatened this utility, not to mention the far more lucrative business of recreation.[15]

The Winton watershed could accommodate almost any outdoor recreational need. Beautiful and remote cabin sites abounded, and wilderness camping and fishing were available for those who wanted a pioneer experience and were willing to travel by canoe. Ely resorts offered experiences across the gamut, from isolated and rustic, with river rock hearths, kerosene lamps, and plain food served to hunters, fishermen, and other backwoods lovers; to family-friendly, with planned activities like nature walks and sunny, sandy beaches; to exclusive, like the Burntside Resort, hosting presidents and serving gourmet game

*Tourism has historically yielded more dollars in Superior National Forest than logging receipts. This canoeist camped along Lake Insula in about 1920.*

banquets. The Boy Scouts and Girl Scouts built camps in the area, and others developed adventure bases and featured canoe trips throughout the BWCA and northwest up to the Arctic. Radios made communication across the wilderness possible, rendering travel much safer and therefore more appealing

By 1948, Ely was the nation's largest freshwater seaplane base, with over twenty-five local operators who made all corners of the lake country accessible in a matter of hours. Remote resorts, wilderness lakes, and backwoods cabins—places that had previously taken days to reach—were suddenly less than an hour from Ely, allowing visitors on even the most restricted timetables to penetrate deep into the wilderness. Outfitters provided all the necessary equipment and guides for any type of trip; visitors needed only their clothes and a pair of good boots, and even these could be purchased in town. Abe Bloomenson's old store, once the lumberjacks' clothier, now sold its Filson, Carhart, and Sheboygan brands to dudes on holiday.[16]

With this ever-increasing tourist traffic and the continued development of industrial logging, the Superior managed a spectrum of opposing interests and seemingly incompatible uses. Those who came for recreation demanded vistas and clean campsites. Hunters sought deer, bear, moose, grouse, and ducks. Fishermen desired fish hatcheries, clean water, and lake access from which to launch boats. Resort owners wanted access roads and long-term leases. Loggers needed roads, fire protection, and trees. But the wilderness idea is not a notion that can brook compromise. Land either is wilderness—held free from motorized contrivance and human industry—or it is not wilderness—governed by the laws of commerce.

Those who came to the Superior for wilderness recreation did not expect to see the burnt stumps and slash of industrial logging, did not want to contend with seaplanes buzzing the lakes or motorboats leaving wakes. They came for peace, quiet, vistas—for spiritual experiences like those of Christopher C. Andrews and Arthur Carhart, for something similar to what Robert Whiteside must have enjoyed as he first paddled the lakes a century earlier. They came for *Quetico*, an Ojibwe word meaning "gentle spirit." The Ojibwe believed that such a spirit inhabits some places and makes them special, that it imbues them with a separate holiness or importance. They considered the border lakes to be one of these places, and many modern visitors shared this assessment. Unlike the push for conservation, which was based on a rational need to protect and conserve a strategic resource, the wilderness idea was a matter of the heart and soul, not of the mind.

Industrial logging threatened this new ethic, and in response people flocked to organizations established to "save" the BWCA. Wilderness activists fought with moral conviction, arguing that recreation produced far more revenue than logging and was thus more important to the local economy. Industry, under the direction of the old union-busting Minnesota Timber Producers Association, exerted intense political pressure so that its members could continue cutting on the BWCA, countering that by building roads for access and by clearing forests, thereby creating habitat for deer and grouse, logging actually enhanced recreational activities. This argument became moot when, in the 1960s, USFS scientists began to urge protection of all remaining virgin tracts in Superior National Forest, many of them within the BWCA. Those who had striven to end logging in the BWCA because they thought it morally repugnant now had not only economic justification but also hard science to back their endeavors.

USFS fire ecologist Dr. Miron "Bud" Heinselman reported that complete fire suppression and industrial logging were compromising forest health, and, more importantly, these activities were also destroying the last remaining undisturbed forest areas, areas invaluable for future scientific study. The BWCA's unlogged land comprised one of the few residual reservoirs of native biological diversity in the east, offering places where the role of fire could be studied effectively and scientists could glimpse what so-called pre-settlement conditions had been. Aldo Leopold stated the problem succinctly when he wrote, "The first rule of intelligent tinkering is to save all the pieces." Heinselman was dismayed to see the few remaining pieces being squandered so quickly and for so little return.

In 1964, against strong, bitter opposition from the timber industry, the Wilderness Act, sponsored by Minnesota senator Hubert Humphrey, created the federal wilderness system and further designated and protected the BWCA, making the area the Boundary Waters

Canoe Area Wilderness (BWCAW). Section 2(a) of the Wilderness Act reads:

> In order to assure that an increasing population, accompanied by expanding settlement and growing mechanization, does not occupy and modify all areas within the United States and its possessions, leaving no lands designated for preservation and protection in their natural condition, it is hereby . . . established a National Wilderness Preservation System to be . . . administered . . . in such manner as will leave them unimpaired for future use and enjoyment as wilderness.[17]

The act goes on to define wilderness as designated federal land "retaining its primeval character and influence, without permanent improvements." But the act contained one of those instances where common sense had to be sacrificed to serve political compromise. Paragraph 4(d)(5) reads:

> Other provisions of this Act to the contrary notwithstanding, the management of the Boundary Waters Canoe Area . . . shall be in accordance with regulations established by the Secretary of Agriculture in accordance with the general principle of maintaining, without unnecessary restrictions on other uses, including that of timber, the primitive character of the area.

Such special treatment was unusual, for in all other wilderness areas designation had meant the end of logging. The lands in question still contained almost two hundred thousand acres of undisturbed but rapidly disappearing forest cover. In 1964, Superior sold virgin trees north of the Echo Trail along Jerry Creek; two years later, Consolidated Paper bought the Old Road block, 2,380 acres of mixed timber east of the old Cloquet line in the Gun, Fairy, Boot, and Fourtown Lakes area; in 1968, Northwest Paper Company acquired the Sunnydale Sale, a five-mile strip of land south of Oyster Lake and west of Ramshead Lake and Lake Agnes. The last timber sale in the wilderness was the Beartrap Sale, to the Kainz brothers, local Winton loggers, 1,150 acres of mixed one-hundred-and-fifty-year-old jack, red, and white pine trees located five miles up the Spring Creek Draw.[18]

In 1974, Heinselman retired from the USFS to devote himself to ending logging in the BWCAW. His final push to complete protection, with the help of other wilderness advocates, was long, bitter, and convoluted, the MTPA vehemently fighting all restrictions. Finally, on October 21, 1978, President Jimmy Carter signed Public Law 95–495, permanently ending logging within the BWCAW.

Forest service bulldozers threw berms across all the roads and removed most culverts, bridges, and dams. With Carter's measure, no vehicles, indeed, no motors of any kind—from chainsaws to snowmobiles to airplanes—were allowed within the wilderness area, the only exceptions being small outboard motors permitted on a few lakes. The old resorts and cabins were closed and the buildings removed. Only a few hardy folks, like Dorothy Molter, known as the Root Beer Lady for the homemade brew she sold to paddlers, remained grandfathered on their homesteads. The legislation was strict: it was illegal to cut any living tree or branch; visitors could gather only downed wood for their campfires; everything packed in had to be packed out again; it was illegal, even, to plant a tree. With the mantra "take nothing but photographs, leave nothing but footprints," Congress had interred the beautiful, myriad, and blessed lakes of the border country behind one of the staunchest legislative walls ever constructed. But what turned out to be the most negative human impact on the land continued despite the wilderness designation: the well-meaning but insidiously destructive fire protection policy.

# 9

## The Big Blow Down

*There are few places left on the North American continent where
men can still see the country as it was before Europeans came
and know some of the challenges and freedoms of those who saw
it first, but in the . . . Northwest it can still be done.*

SIGURD OLSON

---

In the end, the greatest ecological damage to the BWCAW came not from
the lumberjack but from the well-intentioned fledgling foresters trying
to reestablish a timber industry, from their ambitious tree-planting
campaign and their remarkably effective fire-suppression programs.

After the creation of Superior National Forest, the USFS led citizens'
organizations, state conservation agencies, churches, schools, and the
Boy Scouts in planting white pine seedlings in the cutovers around Ely
and Winton. During the depression the Civilian Conservation Corps
(CCC) accelerated this effort. By 1943, more than 32,000 acres of Superior National Forest had been replanted in red, white, and jack pine,
and an additional few thousand acres of state, county, and private lands
had been sown by other agencies and groups. With every hunting li-
cense the state dispensed packets of pine seeds for sportsmen to dis-
tribute as they roamed after grouse, deer, ducks, and bear. Foresters
scattered seed while making their rounds.[1]

Foresters replanted seedlings on more than three thousand acres
within the BWCA. While they grew some seedlings at Birch Lake's nurs-

ery and at others in Eveleth and Two Harbors, many of the trees came from commercial plantations. This flurry of tree planting was not limited to the Winton watershed, for all the Great Lakes states as well as defunct pineries in the east had caught the arbor bug. When American nurseries could not meet demand, groups bought seedlings from European nurseries, mostly in Germany. Some of this seed stock carried the white pine blister rust (*Cronartium ribicola*), a disease well known in Europe, typically causing only minor damage to that continent's white pine. In the United States, however, the disease flourished and was far more destructive.[2]

As early as 1897 scientists in Maine discovered blister rust on English stock of black currant, an alternate host of the disease, but this awareness did not halt import of the foreign seedlings. In 1905 foresters found the rust in Pennsylvania; the following year, in New York. When Congress finally acted against the threat with the Plant Quarantine Act of 1912, it was too late. Three years later, white pine blister rust reached Minnesota, where native flora plus the Arrowhead's weather offered it a particularly accommodating home.[3]

Blister rust spends part of its life on white pine and part on plants belonging to the genus Ribes, such as currants and gooseberries, the latter of which thrives in Minnesota's cutover areas. Blister rust requires both species to reproduce, and its spores can spread from Ribes plants to white pine trees only when the temperature is less than sixty degrees and the pine needles are covered with moisture for at least twenty-four hours. Renowned for cool, still, foggy fall days that come one after another, the border lakes offer perfect conditions for infection. Blister rust zones are rated on a scale from one, where the disease has the least effective reproduction and spread, to four, where the disease is most destructive. The Arrowhead sets the top of the scale.

Fire suppression only contributed to the spread and intensification of the disease. White pine regeneration depends on periodic low-intensity fire to clear competing plants from beneath the overstory. Such fire also suppresses Ribes plants by consuming the litter on the forest floor, wiping out not only the plant but also its seed bank stored there. The dense undergrowth that flourishes in the absence of fire increases blister rust infection by trapping moisture near the ground, by crowding and stressing pine seedlings, and by creating denser concentrations of Ribes.

Fire has always been part of white pine's growing cycle. Historically, moderate-intensity fires crept through the northern forests about once every thirty to fifty years, destroying Ribes seeds, burning the leaf litter, and leaving mineral soils exposed. White pine seed will only take hold when it is in direct contact with mineral soils; without periodic fires to clear the forest floor, very few sites had exposed soils on which the seedlings could establish themselves. Fire also tends to move quickly up hills, burning less intensely and with less scorch, releasing seed source without damaging older pine trees. Especially after the introduction of blister rust, pine tends to do better on these slopes as opposed to low-lying areas, where cool air and moisture settle, making for higher infection rates.

Although fire would have helped white pine fight off the intruder, the CCC, the Works Progress Administration, the USFS, and state agencies took a different tack. In the 1930s and 1940s, many of the same groups that had planted seedlings with such enthusiasm a decade earlier undertook an enormous campaign to eradicate Ribes, destroying acre-by-acre every gooseberry plant they discovered. Miserable work, it was also futile. Thorny and tenacious, gooseberries are difficult to pull, and they can sprout again from even small fragments left in the rocky soil or a branch dropped on the way to the burn pile. By the 1940s, researchers feared that infection rates were as high as 99 percent in some areas of the BWCA, although later scientists lowered this figure somewhat. Blister rust continued to spread, and in the early 1950s, after spending an estimated $100 million on the project, the forest service gave up its effort.[4]

Blister rust typically doesn't kill older trees. Remnant white pine are strong enough to survive the epidemic, showing signs of infection—dead, skeletal limbs and tops, known as "flags"—but continuing to produce and scatter seed. The seeds do well in areas where fire has kept the competing fir and aspen trees to a minimum and exposed the soil. In some areas white pine seedlings carpet the forest floor, fernlike, around their ancient parents. These seedlings are not living to adulthood, however. Blister rust can only travel a short distance from where it infects a tree, at the needle, and so on older trees only kills limbs, never reaching and girdling the trunk. In younger trees, where the distance from needle to trunk is less, white pine mortality is much higher.

Today, Superior's white pine are either old, remnant, pre-infection trees or very young trees. Healthy middle-aged trees are rare. The white pine component of the forest had diminished so far and reproduction rates become so low that in 1986 the USFS changed the forest classification from Great Lakes pine forest to aspen/hardwood forest. Still, even hampered by disease, white pine probably would have begun to reestablish itself on the land had it not been for fire suppression efforts, which were absolute.

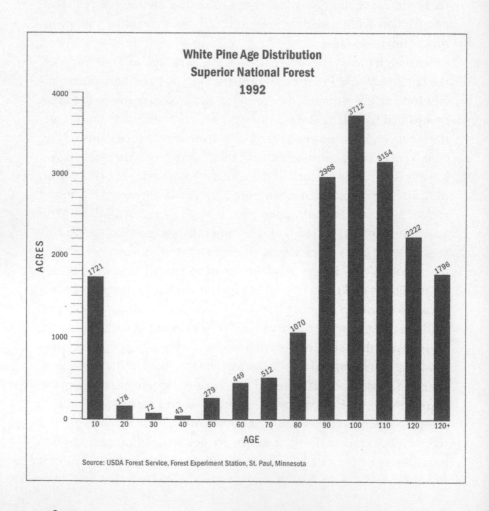

Source: USDA Forest Service, Forest Experiment Station, St. Paul, Minnesota

In the terrible fire year of 1910, five million acres of national forest burned. One fire in Idaho killed seventy-nine firefighters and burned three million acres in forty-eight hours. During that fire, a prospector turned forest ranger, Edward Pulaski, had a 150-man crew defending the town of Wallace. The hurricane of flame bore down on them so quickly that Pulaski could gather only forty-five of his men, leading them to a mineshaft he remembered. Pulaski held his panicked men in the burning mine at gunpoint. Only five died, and Pulaski became a national hero. In response to the tragedy, the nation declared war on wildland fire. For nearly a century federal, state, and county agencies fought an unrelenting battle against fire in all corners of the country. Their efforts produced immediate results, as the size and intensity of wildland fires dropped. During the dry, windy summer of 1919, what promised to be a bad fire year, only 2.5 million acres of national forestland burned, even though the forest service managed far more land then it had in 1910. In 1926, another dry year, less than a million acres of national forests burned; after 1934, thanks to CCC efforts, the average was less than three hundred thousand acres a year. In the forest service's

*Enrollees of the Civilian Conservation Corps weed white spruce seedlings at the Knife River Nursery in 1940, preparing the trees for eventual transplant in the national forests.*

early years, the typical fire burned about one hundred acres, but by the 1940s this average had dropped to just thirty-one.[5]

As CCC laborers made almost all of Superior National Forest accessible by road, nearly every acre could be watched throughout fire season. In 1934, the service adopted the policy, "Every fire out by 10:00 A.M. of the day following its report," and it fairly well met that ambitious goal. In Montana, the USFS established a firefighting school that turned out crews of elite smoke jumpers, people in top physical condition who parachuted into even the most remote fires, extinguishing them in their infancy. Into accessible areas the USFS sent forty-person teams, hotshot crews, trained to fight major campaigns against large blazes. Fire, whether caused by man or by nature, was almost completely snuffed out across the continent, North America becoming virtually fireproof for the first time since a two-mile-thick sheet of ice had covered it.

Warnings from Smokey the Bear, coupled with the 1942 Disney movie *Bambi* and its terrible fire scene, reinforced the public's negative view of fire and inspired change. Even in remote areas, where rural Americans had long used fire to clear land, destroy waste, heat homes, cook food, prepare fields, and clean drainage ditches, firefighting took on patriotic overtones. The new war against fire was complete: pastoral America exchanged fire for machinery, pesticides, and herbicides. Following World War II utility companies made electricity available across the continent, introducing gas and electric ranges and heaters to replace wood cook stoves and hearths in isolated homes and cabins. Fire in the home became an ornament or symbol rather than a necessity; some Americans even lost the skill to build a fire without matches or other incendiary.

Following the Korean War, many of the surplus planes, earthmovers, and even soldiers were reassigned to the nation's war on wildland fire. Fire crews outfitted planes and helicopters with large scoops or buckets, and daring pilots learned to gather water "on the fly," skimming nearby lakes or rivers for ammunition to "bomb" the flames. The service eventually developed a flame-retardant gel that pilots sprayed from tanker planes onto buildings to protect them from out-of-control blazes. Firefighters herded the fires that got away, protecting towns and cities, holding death rates and the number of destroyed homes to almost zero for many years.

Grasslands no longer blazed in the early spring and late fall, and trees invaded open spaces from Ohio to Iowa. In the west, ponderosa pine communities grew up in thickets. Lodgepole and jack pine forests began to deteriorate and then to topple without fire to re-establish them by melting the sticky resin that seals and protects the trees' cones and thus their seed. The number of acres destroyed by wildfire tumbled. In 1973, fewer than two million acres went up in smoke nationwide. The forests were virtually fireproof.

But in the 1960s Superior National Forest fire ecologist Bud Heinselman broke ranks. He had determined that in health the BWCAW is not static but is a changing landscape, like so many of nature's patterns—shifting sand dunes, waves rolling onto a beach, winds through tall grass, flames off a log, churning thunderheads, lifting fog—all similar in structure and shape but each unique, infinitely variable, a mosaic. The engine that drove the BWCAW system, that determined the overall patterns—the species types and distributions and ages—was fire. Like the surface of a pond in constant motion from invisible breezes, so fire acted on the landscape of the BWCAW, keeping it moving within a specific predictable pattern, what ecologists call a Historic Range of Natural Variability (HRNV).

The HRNV pattern in the BWCAW evolved very slowly, requiring about three hundred years to show its many faces on any given acre. Some susceptible areas probably experienced a stand-replacing fire once every thirty years, while at the opposite end of the spectrum pines growing on small islands or along leeward lakeshores, protected by water or wetlands, might burn completely only once every five hundred years.

Different types of fires create or promote assorted species in the BWCAW. Stand-killing crown fires, like those following logging operations, tend to scorch the earth and kill red and white pine seed stock and cones. These same high temperatures, however, are required to melt the amberlike resin of jack pine. Creeping fires release the shade-tolerant white pine, burn out competition, and leave a pine canopy that not only retains soil moisture and encourages future creeping fires but also drowns out sun-dependent aspen and jack pine, which burn more readily. In areas where fire destroys a stand, aspen can restock with as many as forty thousand stems per acre. If creeping fires intrude, flaring up periodically and killing the crown, more shade-tolerant species like white pine, balsam fir, or spruce move in depending on the opening's size, the site's moisture, and the soil type. In areas where disease or insect infestation destroys a stand, fire typically kills the host trees and curtails the epidemic.

*The forest service's efforts to reduce the number and intensity of forest fires saw results in the decades after a 1934 fire burned areas of Cass and Itasca Counties, its path of destruction shown in this* St. Paul Dispatch *photograph.*

The forest service froze this mosaic when it extinguished wildfires, and this policy, more than any other human activity, caused the greatest long-term harm to the system. Fire, argued Heinselman, was not a destructive or negative force in the BWCAW forest but was actually beneficial and necessary. His findings were a hard sell, however; after decades of fire suppression, the idea that land managers should set wildfires was an impossible heresy.

In the fireless forest, stands of early successional species like aspen, spruce, and balsam—which would have burned in earlier times—grew to the end of their life cycles, deteriorated, and died. Aspen and jack pine followed the flames now, not cedar, white spruce, or pine. These extremely flammable species grew under the few remaining stands of old white pine, the smaller trees fairly exploding when the infrequent creeping ground fires reached them. Flames flashed up into the canopy pines, reached the crowns where winds were stronger, and wiped out remaining old-growth stands, trees that would have once benefited from the flames. Before European incursion, fuel loads in the BWCAW probably averaged fewer than five tons per acre. After nearly a century of fire suppression efforts, fuels had built to twenty tons per acre. These larger fuel loads, comprised of downed wood or standing young flammable trees, resulted in fewer light creeping fires, replaced by more intense, less controllable fires. Gary Brown, wilderness fire manager for the BWCAW, said, "We have loaded fuels to the point where fires in the wilderness have gone from periodic low intensity fires to where all fire in the wilderness is now a stand-replacing fire."[6]

The USFS and other federal agencies like the National Park Service, the Bureau of Land Management, and the Bureau of Indian Affairs refused to give up the war on wildfire. Budgets depended on putting out flames, not on lighting fires. The public, having adopted Smokey the Bear's message, was reluctant to abandon the idea that fire was destructive. While Superior National Forest tinkered with prescribed burns on small lots, the BWCAW remained fireless.

The Wilderness Act directed foresters to manage the area first for "natural integrity," that is, in a way that would preserve the area's long-term ecological processes. Section 2(a) of the act, passed on September 3, 1964, dictates: "these [wilderness areas] shall be administered for the use and enjoyment of the American people in such manner as will leave them unimpaired for future use and enjoyment as wilderness." Section 2(c) provides a helpful definition: "A wilderness, in contrast with those areas where man and his own works dominate . . . [is an] area of undeveloped Federal land retaining its primeval character and influence, without permanent improvements or human habitation, which is protected and managed so as to preserve its natural conditions."

Under this authority, Heinselman and others urged forest managers to set low-intensity ground fires and to allow lightning-caused fires to run their course, arguing that this was the only way to protect and manage the land "so as to preserve its natural conditions." Heinselman wrote: "combining prescribed-controlled fire with carefully selected and monitored lightning fires, is the only alternative for the Canoe Area that responds to the objective of restoring the natural ecosystem with safety . . . no road construction or use of tractors would be allowed [in the work]." This last bit of advice was a nod to the act's instruction that management of the land should occur so that it "generally appears to have been affected primarily by the forces of nature, with the imprint of man's work substantially unnoticed." Forest supervisors, however, determined that in order to comply with the Wilderness Act all fires must be suppressed.[7]

The Wilderness Act further stipulates that human activity is not to be visible to the average visitor, that "outstanding opportunities for solitude" exist, and that visitors have the opportunity to be isolated from the sights, sounds, and presence of other humans; that there be "outstanding opportunities for primitive recreation," a "vastness of scale," a sense that one is part of the natural environment, and a degree of challenge and risk for the average visitor. In response to the law, wilderness land management inside the BWCAW became focused on the recreational rather than the ecological, while outside the wilderness area timber production continued to dominate forest service activities. Setting fire seemed to conflict with these other directives, so the service continued its "every fire out by 10:00" policy. With the passing decades, policies changed very little and fuel loads built higher in the BWCAW and across the country.

Finally, as each year saw an increase in the average number of acres burned, fire began to win the battle. Managers realized that, despite heroic effort and the latest technology, mounting fuel loads made wildfire inevitable. By 1986, forest managers on the Superior had responded to this increasing threat with a policy known as "Wildland Fire Use for Resource Benefits." The plan differentiated between lightning-caused fires and fires started by humans, allowing "natural" fires to burn but directing that all human-caused fires be extinguished immediately. Despite good intentions, under the new policy only ten percent of the BWCAW burned from 1986 to 1996, a level far below historic rates and much too low to substantially reduce fuel loads or to mitigate other ecological problems caused by fire suppression.[8]

In the 1990s fire began to reassert itself across the American landscape. Five of the worst fire years since 1960 darkened skies in that decade. Fuel loads had reached a level at which not all fires could be contained. Cities were expanding, bringing people within close proximity of the forests once again: all the corridors into the BWCAW and many adjacent lakes were being developed with homes, cabins, and resorts. Wilderness was becoming extraordinarily popular, both as a destination and as a symbol of environmental commitment. More people were in the woods at a time when fires were becoming less predictable, placing human life increasingly at risk.

On October 21, 1991, a brush fire crept off public wildlands and into the Oakland Hills above San Francisco Bay. Low humidity and high winds quickly spread the fire up the dry, duff- and scrub-filled canyon. Almost eight hundred buildings, mostly beautiful upper-income suburban homes, burned in the first hour alone. Indians had once flamed these steep, dry hills to improve habitat for game. The land had been oak savanna, well stocked with ungulates, but pioneers cut the oaks and misguided settlers planted eucalyptus, thinking the wood would be good for railroad ties or construction. While eucalyptus never proved commercially valuable, it was prodigious, and the resinous, shaggy-barked, and highly flammable tree spread across the hills. Suburbanites, wanting a semi-rural setting where they could escape the crush of the city yet live close enough to work there, built luxury homes, many with cedar-shingled roofs and wooden decks, among the trees. The homes that spread up the Oakland Hills in the 1980s invaded an increasingly flammable forest, a zone fire ecologists now call the Wildland/Urban Interface.

In 1994, another bad fire year, thirty-four firefighters died—the most since 1910—two million acres burned, and costs rose to a staggering $965 million. The federal wildland fire agencies hired a consulting firm to assess the situation. In addition to meteorologists and fire specialists, the firm interviewed hotshots and smoke jumpers from around the country. The number one threat firefighters described was fuel accumulation due to fire suppression.

After 1994, burn specialists and ecologists used potential loss of life and property to leverage a prescribed burn policy for Superior National Forest. Supervisors began to allow some burning, but narrow interpretations of the Wilderness Act prevented ecologists from setting fires inside the BWCAW. Even outside the wilderness managers were cautious, burning no more than two thousand acres a year on the Superior. While these fires did have some ecological benefit, protection of property determined the burns' location, with managers creating low fuel areas, so-called black lines, between the wilderness and people. One example is the Gunflint Trail, which snakes into the wilderness and places thousands of homes, resorts, and small settlements in the path of catastrophe. To protect these people and their dwellings, fire specialists began setting defensive fires to serve as breaks to blazes coming in from the southwest.[9]

The USFS began a public relations program to educate locals on the benefits of the prescribed burn policy. But their efforts came to naught when the National Park Service set a fire to address high fuel loads in the mountains of Los Alamos, New Mexico, and rangers lost control of the blaze, declaring it a wildfire on May 5, 2000. Two days later officials began evacuating the citizens of Los Alamos, home to the world's largest nuclear laboratory. The nation watched as flames entered the city and held its collective breath in anticipation of what promised to be a mighty cataclysm. The fires destroyed almost four hundred homes and displaced nearly twenty-five thousand people, but valiant firefighters managed to stop the blaze a mere three hundred yards from the plutonium storage facility at the Los Alamos National Laboratory.

National attention riveted on the issue of wildfire. Wildfires the country over were not only more numerous but were burning hotter, faster, and higher—indeed, all fires were becoming catastrophic. Many western legislators transparently suggested logging as an alternative to controlled burns, ignoring the true source of the problem, that past logging—removing large fire-tolerant trees—and fire suppression had created the high fuel loads in the first place.[10]

After Los Alamos, more of the public had misgivings about setting fires, especially in a wilderness area. The average person still viewed fire, not fuels, as the problem. People feared fire would destroy the recreational utility of the BWCAW, which had become a very precious commodity indeed. Beginning in the 1980s, wilderness recreation values in the BWCAW were the highest in the nation. In 2001, 282,043 people visited the BWCAW, spending on average $128.14 within fifty miles of the wilderness for a positive economic impact of over $36 million that year alone. Some feared that fire would consume tourism dollars. Superior National Forest fire specialist Paul Tiné noted that the Los Alamos fire "made life hard for everybody because suddenly the public was saying, 'Oh my God, every time you drop a match the world is going to burn up.'" Forester supervisors remained cautious and took no action.[11]

In addition to a frightened public, the USFS also faced budgetary concerns. Much of the money earmarked for setting prescribed burns was being consumed by fighting wildfire. Even as uncontrollable fires were becoming an increasing threat, more people were moving into Wildland/Urban Interfaces like Oakland Hills. These ex-urbanites, living in unincorporated communities with no local fire protection, relied on federal agencies like the Forest Service or the Bureau of Land Management to protect them. Not only was the fire danger greater, but these new rural populations, living on the edge of wilderness, made it far more likely that both people and property would be consumed. Protecting private holdings from wildfires drained monies intended for prescribed fires and made the job of reducing fuel loads far more complicated.[12]

As the Wildland Fire Use Rule remained in force, budget-starved prescribed burn plans languished and fire-famished ecosystems choked on fuel. Ecologists and fire specialists like Tiné continued quietly writing a new prescribed burn policy to include in a revision of the Superior National Forest Plan, a guide to all management decisions, updated every fifteen years. In 1999, as the Forest Plan neared completion and shortly before its release for what was sure to be a contentious period of public comment, nature forced the issue, effectively ending the debate.

July 4, 1999, was a hot, humid day in northern Minnesota. As the afternoon wore on the barometric pressure built and anvil clouds boiled higher in the western sky. A squall line emerged across the horizon and the storm raced forward, sending sheets of rain, lightning, and high winds before it. Wind-tossed torrents flooded the landscape, and a wall cloud, sharp and flat, like a thousand-foot scythe blade, hung poised above the heart of the BWCAW. The sky, the very air itself, became turquoise green, subterranean. Then the scythe fell. The wall of wind-driven water rolled over on itself like a wave and broke, sweeping at speeds up to 120 miles an hour across a twenty-mile-wide corridor from Rainy Lake to the Gunflint Trail. The wind did not gust but remained steady, wavering only slightly in direction but not in intensity, driving frothy ten-foot whitecaps across lakes. For twelve long seconds the sharp wind screamed, and then it relented. In its passing, 40 million trees had been snapped off or uprooted and toppled.[13]

Almost seven inches of rain fell that afternoon. Four hundred thousand acres of trees lay tumbled across the wilderness on the American side of the border, an additional one hundred thousand acres on the Canadian side. Although there were about 2,500 people in the wilderness when the storm hit, no one died. Many were injured, and more were trapped on lakes, the portage trails buried under as much as thirty feet of tangled blow down. Emergency search and rescue and trail clearing lasted about two weeks. After this, one of the largest blow downs ever recorded in North America, the average fuel load on the BWCAW jumped from twenty to over one hundred tons per acre, 120 times historic levels.[14]

Even those staunchly opposed to the practice had always recognized that the Wilderness Act requires managers to ignite prescribed burns when at least one of the following criteria exists: fuel treatment measures outside the wilderness are not sufficient to meet fire management objectives within the wilderness, an interdisciplinary team of resource specialists has evaluated and recommended the use of fire, the public has been involved in the decision, and lightning-caused fires pose a threat to life or property. Wildfire experts reported that the BWCAW's huge fuel loads meant lightning was far more likely to strike dry fuel and start a fire under a wider variety of conditions and that the resulting fires were apt to be much larger than the most significant fires of old. Because of increased fuel density, experts predicted a higher spread rate under even moderate weather conditions of low wind and high humidity. Most startling was the increased likelihood of a plume-dominated fire, like those of Hinckley and the Big Blowup.

Plume-dominated fires create their own weather, with smoke columns reaching 30,000 to 50,000 feet high. Strong indrafts on the fire perimeter can quickly change to forty-mile-an-hour downdrafts. Fire whirls, literally balls of flame, calve along the perimeter and roll out into the countryside, starting spot fires up to three miles away. Plume-dominated fires are hurricanes of flame driven by fuel and their own internal mechanisms. They can move in any direction regardless of prevailing winds and so are totally unpredictable, unfightable, unmanageable maelstroms.[15]

Suddenly the USFS simply could not let a single fire burn, regardless of how it started. Any wildfire in the BWCAW would be cataclysmic and could easily escape the wilderness, burning out homes and businesses along the Gunflint or Echo Trails or in Ely and Winton. Now that the BWCAW was the world's largest bonfire, awaiting only a match or lightning strike, the debate over prescribed burns was over. Fire had forced itself back onto the landscape. In May 2001, forest supervisor Jim Sanders, who had helped manage the 1988 Yellowstone fires, seized upon the burning plan Tiné and forest ecologists had been drafting. "Fires we expect are far better than fires we don't expect," reasoned Sanders at open meetings sponsored by the forest service. The public, eyeing stacked fuels in the wilderness, readily agreed.

Because budget restrictions had forced Tiné to justify earlier burns by claiming they would protect property outside the BWCAW, his prescribed burn plan needed very little adjustment to mitigate the danger posed by the blow down. The *Environmental Impact Statement* and *Fuel*

*Treatment Record of Decision* the USFS released preempted wildfire by setting small fires in a checkerboard pattern just west of heavily populated areas, like the Gunflint and Echo Trails and west of Trout Lake. Any fire sweeping across the wilderness from southwest to northeast, the direction of prevailing winds, would meet areas where the fuel was broken up and so decrease in intensity or go out altogether. The plan scheduled burns in the early spring and late fall, when the relative humidity and temperatures were such that the fires would not burn as hot. Not only are cooler fires safer, they are more ecologically beneficial as well. The burn specialists and interdisciplinary scientific panel Sanders assembled proposed setting seventy-nine separate fires, burning a total of 75,605 acres.

Sanders also crafted a plan to cut and clear almost 193 miles of fire control line to prevent blazes from escaping and burning in unintended areas. In this way, after approximately seven years of lighting smaller fires when weather conditions are best for controlling them, the service hopes to, "create a situation in the wilderness in which we can effectively contain wildfires and again allow lightning-ignited fire to burn [Wildland Fire Use]." The goal of the prescribed burn is to "improve public safety by reducing the potential for high-intensity Wildland fires to spread from the BWCAW into areas . . . containing homes, cabins, resorts, and other improvements and areas across the international border into Canada." Still, once the threat from the blow down has been lessened, the USFS has no plan to continue lighting prescribed fires inside the wilderness. The Wildland Fire Use rule still stands.[16]

While the July 4 winds were naturally occurring and blow downs have happened periodically in the BWCAW, the scale of the storm's destruction was far out of proportion to anything in the past, the devastation increased by the effects of wilderness management philosophies on the landscape, most notably, fire suppression. Logging and fire suppression have converted much of the BWCAW to an aspen/hardwood forest. Where once this region was dominated by white, red, and jack pine,

OPPOSITE:
*Decades of fire suppression, logging, and blister rust enabled the straight-line winds of July 4, 1999, to blow down acres of trees in the boundary waters area on both sides of the U.S.–Canada border.*

today these trees are becoming increasingly rare, or, in the case of white pine, nearly extinct. Aspen, the new dominant species, is unfortunately one of the most susceptible to blow downs. Dr. Lee Frelich, a disturbance ecologist at the University of Minnesota, asserts that periodic fire would have created a mosaic of stand types and age classes so that even the strong winds of July 4, 1999, might not have caused such uniform and continuous destruction. The aspen and jack pine that grew up in the wake of logging, shielded from fire, were all ripe for wind throw at the same time. Younger, more flexible stands would have survived, as would have dense stands of older white and red pine.[17]

The blow down proved that constructing a legislative wall around a piece of land protects it only from industry. When the trees fell in the nation's first and most popular wilderness area, for many the wilderness phase of land management ended, to be replaced by a new paradigm: restoration. However, the answer to the question, "restore to what?" proves to be surprisingly complicated.

# Epilogue

*Only to the white man was nature a "wilderness" and only to him was the land "infested" with "wild" animals and "savage" people.*

LUTHER STANDING BEAR (1868–1939),
Chief of the Oglala Sioux

---

SEPTEMBER 16, 2002, was a perfect autumn day in the Boundary Waters: the sky clear, relative humidity about 50 percent, winds light at less than ten miles per hour. Quicksilver dewdrops clung to amber leaves and drying grass. Nearly all of the cabin folk had closed up and gone home; the resorts were mostly vacant; shutters covered the windows. Skeletal docks hung tilted out of the water like singular lift bridges, raised to prevent them from being swept away by the ice that would soon fill the lakes. Overnight frost had knocked down most of the buzzing and biting insects, but temperatures promised to reach seventy-five by late afternoon, perfect for autumn picnics, for long walks among the changing leaves, for watching migrating birds, for late fall fishing. At Magnetic Lake, where the Gunflint Trail ends, about fifty outboards dotted the calm water. The boats were filled not with fishermen, however, but with USFS hotshots in flame-retardant Day-Glo yellow Nomex shirts. The Lunds were loaded to the gunwales with wilderness firefighting tools—pumps, hoses, shovels, chainsaws, and blunt and savage pulaskis.

These characters and their props suggested impending catastrophe, and the woods on this peaceful, lovely day were far from quiet or empty. Pump trucks and local volunteer firefighters stood parked and ready at the pull offs along the north end of the Gunflint Trail, the dirt two lane that arcs far into the eastern end of the wilderness area. In resort parking lots, lights flashed from EMT trucks and ambulances, army reservist Hummers, and search-and-rescue vehicles. Police cruisers, gumballs revolving, patrolled each infrequent intersection. Still, the scene lacked urgency, as if the fine fall day had lulled the emergency crews into complacency. Cops stood smoking beside their vehicles. Emergency workers sat in trucks or vans, talking, drinking coffee, and munching donuts. The hotshot crews on Magnetic Lake let their boats drift in the light breeze, napping on coiled bundles of hose, life preservers, and water bladders. Some formed small flotillas. Everyone waited, poised but inactive. The sun climbed higher. The relative humidity dropped. The dew began to dry.

At about ten o'clock, five hotshots landed on a small island just off the mainland shore and climbed from the boat. A mock chalet, with Swiss gabled roofs and elf statuary, a fantasy, what the British call a "folly," squatted in the middle of a manicured lawn on the little island. The crew started a massive sprinkler system mounted on the cedar-shingled roof, veils of water soon covering the garish elf statues, the leaded windows, the slate paths, the cedar hot tub and wooden decks. The fire crew retreated just beyond the drifting spray and stood smoking. The day grew warmer.

Then the bass, subsonic *thump, thump, thump* of powerful helicopter blades slicing the cool morning air shattered the quiet. The hotshot crews on Magnetic Lake turned to watch as three Bell 206 helicopters rose above the ridge on the western shore like predatory drones, advancing on the wilderness in attack formation. Swinging on long cables below the Bells were heliotorches, fifty-five-gallon drums of gasoline mixed with detergent—homemade napalm—outfitted with a simple torch and sprayer. The copters flew to the north shore of the wilderness lake just beyond the mansion, hovered there, and then sent a shower of flame cascading down upon the BWCAW.

Plumes of white smoke rose almost immediately, within a few minutes turning a dark black. The helicopters' swirling rotors caught and churned the thick fume, engulfing the aircraft, forcing a retreat by degrees, the burning rain pouring from the heliotorches onto the wilderness. Then the barrels were empty. The Bells swung away northwest, in formation. Three others advanced to continue the assault. The smoke formed a solid column, straight and dense and impenetrable, a convection plume. It rose to three thousand feet, then five thousand, then higher. The flames glowed within the tower of black smoke, animating the destruction. Support aircraft, three De Haviland Beavers, and the command platform, a Cessna 182, circled the pillar of smoke.

On the ground the fire spread greedily. Whole trees caught at once and exploded with flame, sending showers of crackling bark, burning wood shards, and resinous pinecones shooting hundreds of feet into the sky. The roar of fire became deafening, drowning out even the helicopters, like the sound of a freight train, or a wind tunnel, or a jet engine.

*In 2002, the forest service modified its long-held policy of complete fire suppression when it set prescribed burns in the BWCAW to mitigate fuel loads left in the wake of a severe windstorm. This fire burned near Griddle Lake.*

Still the crews sat idly, more attentive but inactive. The hotshots at the gingerbread mansion edged out to the very end of the dock.

This massive collection of human and emergency resources had been sent north to burn the wilderness, not to save it. Unless the fire escaped the parameters set forth in the prescription, they would do nothing. So began a new phase in the evolving drama between humans and the northern Minnesota border lakes region. Setting the three-thousand-acre Magnetic Lake fire inside the BWCAW was the first practical expression of an emerging management paradigm: restoration forestry.

Fire finally forced land managers to abandon many of the primary assumptions they once held regarding land and to violate previously sacrosanct rules. The threat of catastrophic wildfire obliged the USFS to take a more active hand in managing the border lakes wilderness. Still, burn plans will treat only the fuel loads from the July 4, 1999, storm, ending after the forest service has burned the 74,000 acres required to mitigate the blow-down fuels. There is no plan to set ecologically motivated wildfire in the BWCAW. Protection of private property is the only legitimized goal, and two years were required for the USFS to take even that halting, cumbersome step. Still, the Magnetic Lake burn opened the door a crack. Using prescribed fire for ecological benefits may soon happen. The same helicopters that drop flame could also drop disease-resistant white pine seeds.

The incredible destruction of the July 4, 1999, blow down demonstrated Heinselman's argument that total fire exclusion is a misguided notion. Even the practice of Wildland Fire Use—letting lightning-ignited fires burn and eradicating "unnatural" or anthropomorphic fires—did not break up the even-aged stands that blew down in the July 4 storm or reduce fuel loads to the point where catastrophic wildfire no longer posed a threat. Essay writer Wendell Berry phrases the dilemma well:

> "In wilderness is the preservation of the world," as Thoreau said, may be a spiritual truth, but it is also a practical fact.
> On the other hand, we must not fail to consider the opposite proposition—that, so long at least as humans are in the world, in human culture is the preservation of wildness—which is equally and more demandingly, true. If wildness is to survive, then we must preserve it.

Berry could well have written, "If wildness is to survive, then we must *restore* it." Wildness, as it is used here, seems to describe a forest that has not been degraded by humans. Restoration presupposes human involvement and management of a system, even a "pristine wilderness," and at first glance seems contradictory. But anthropomorphic fire was a part of the wildness that modern life has suppressed. Manmade fire is an integral part of a wild, natural landscape.[1]

The 2003 Draft Superior National Forest Plan recognizes this, stating, "It is . . . necessary to develop management direction that incorporates ecosystem processes, such as the role of prescribed fire." But restoring fire to an ecosystem demands that managers answer some difficult questions. The Forest Plan continues, "Current Forest Plans do not recognize fire as an essential ecological process in forest management. . . . There is a need to reconsider direction for fire management and address fire in an ecological context."[2]

This philosophy pertains only to national forestlands outside the BWCAW. The 2003 Forest Plan specifically states that there will be no change in the BWCAW's fire policy, still defined by the Wildland Fire rule, which allows only natural fires to burn. Setting fires is a more difficult concept, for the dilemma becomes when and how much to burn, a question of goals or agendas that are not always easy to define. Scientists like Lee Frelich look to the Historic Range of Natural Variability for guidance. By studying charcoal layers in the soils of the BWCAW, Bud Heinselman discovered that before European incursion about ten thousand acres had burned inside the wilderness boundaries each year. Under the USFS Wildland Fire Use Rule, initiated in 1987, "naturally" ignited fires consumed on average only fifteen hundred acres annually, logically inspiring the question: how, historically, did the other 8,500 acres burn? The answer reveals a deep and almost universal cultural bias.

The idea that Aboriginal Americans were few in number and lived in roving bands hunting and gathering a providential bounty, that they lived in harmony with nature, that their impact on the environment was negligible at most and benign at least, is one of the cornerstones of western environmental thought. It is also without much corroborative evidence.

Most histories of the Americas begin in 1492, with the aboriginals cast either as tragic Adams and Eves or as unfortunate obstacles to progress, their stories swept aside in favor of Euro-centric perspectives. Only recently have historians, aided by anthropologists, archaeologists, botanists, ecologists, geneticists, and even foresters, begun to paint a picture of America that includes an accurate and detailed account of the aboriginals that once lived here and the impact they had on the ecosystems Europeans found. The far-reaching implications of these more detailed histories call into question some of our culture's most popular myths. Aboriginal Americans managed their environment intensively, at the landscape scale and with a great degree of sophistication. What whites discovered when they arrived in the New World was not a bountiful natural providence in balance but a cultural artifact, the carefully designed and managed landscapes of a people recently deceased or rapidly vanishing.

Anthropologists and archaeologists have been increasing estimates of the number of people who lived in the Americas before European settlement. Currently a hot debate surrounds the exact number, but no one contests the overall trend. There were far more Indians than historians have traditionally believed, and they managed the land far more intensively than anyone had previously imagined.

In 1910 the Smithsonian's James Mooney established a population of 1.48 million people for all of North America and Mexico in 1491. Mooney didn't account for epidemic disease, however, which often wiped out villages before whites encountered them. Aboriginal Americans had little or no resistance to European diseases, and epidemics, when they hit these "virgin soil populations"—people who have never been infected by a particular pathogen—were extremely vicious. The first Europeans who traveled to the Americas typically left no record of their journeys, no letters to describe what they found, no demographic estimates, no journals or logs. They did, however, carry smallpox, bubonic plague, measles, mumps, influenza, cholera, typhoid, and whooping cough. Most Aboriginal Americans died long before they had met any European, long before early chroniclers could compile population statistics, long before most Europeans even knew they had existed.[3]

The Pilgrims during their first year encountered a number of abandoned villages and fallow fields but saw only a few Aboriginal Americans, and those at a distance. One Pilgrim, having reconnoitered the surrounding countryside, told ghastly tales of finding towns where Indian skulls and bones lay strewn about above ground, reminding him of Golgotha. The following spring, the Pilgrims finally met an aboriginal, Squanto. William Bradford wrote in his journal on March 16, 1621:

> He saluted us in English and bade us welcome. He had learned some broken English amongst Englishmen that came to fish at Monhegan and knew by name most of the captains, commanders, and masters of ships which usually come. He told us the place we now live is called Patuxet. About four years ago all the inhabitants died of an extraordinary plague. There is neither man, woman, nor child remaining, as indeed we have found none, so that there is now none to hinder our possession or lay claim to it.

The epidemic, probably viral hepatitis, took years to exhaust itself, killing 90 percent of the aboriginals living in costal New England before the Pilgrims landed on Plymouth Rock.[4]

Fourteen years after Mooney established his figure of 1.48 million, anthropologist H. J. Spinder revised it upwards to reflect his belief that several million people had lived in the east alone. Much later, in 1976, Henry Dobyns, who has compiled the most detailed studies of Aboriginal American demographics to date, wrote:

> The Americas were densely populated at the time Europeans found their way to this New World. Recent estimates place the hemispheric population at 100,000,000 in about 1490. Perhaps two-fifths of that total inhabited North America, including the civilized states in Mexico (which contained 30,000,000 people). Native Americans achieved those densities because they inhabited a relatively disease-free paradise and domesticated high-yield cereals and tubers.

More than ninety-three deadly epidemics and pandemics raged through Aboriginal American populations from the 1500s to 1900, killing 80 percent or more of the people in the first onslaught and in some cases 95 percent of a population in a single episode. David E. Stannard, professor of American Studies at the University of Hawaii, writes, "demographers have been uncovering . . . post-Columbian depopulation rates of between 90 and 98 percent with such regularity that an overall decline of 95 percent has become a working rule of thumb."[5]

Recently, some researchers have adjusted Dobyns's population figures to 145 million for the western hemisphere, with about 18 million people living in North America. While determining hard numbers is difficult and there is much dissention about the actual figures, all agree that far more people lived in the Americas in 1491 than has been reported in the past, probably more than lived in Europe at the same time.[6]

Americans have traditionally underestimated not only the number of people living on this continent before European incursion but also the impact these people had, their relationship with the environment, and the degree to which they changed the world around them to suit their needs. The answer to how the extra 8,500 acres in the BWCAW burned before white settlement was hidden beneath a blanket-like cultural bias. Not only were anthropomorphic fires "natural" in the BWCAW, aboriginal burning most likely established and maintained the basic ecological patterns of the border lakes long before Europeans arrived. Omer Stewart, an anthropologist working in the 1950s, wrote:

> the question remains as to whether the northeastern pine forest, which extended for a thousand miles from northern Minnesota through southern Ontario and Quebec to the Gulf of St. Lawrence, resulted from fires started by lightning or from fires set by Indians. . . . This interpretation appears necessary in view of the great extent of the territory and in view of the relative unimportance of lightning in the area . . . lightning is seldom the cause of forest fires east of the Rocky Mountains. . . . Thus the great area burned and the relative infrequency of forest fires caused by lightning strongly suggest that Indian fires were a primary factor in the formation of jack, red, and white pine forests of the northeastern United States and Canada.[7]

For thousands of years, first the Dakota and then the Ojibwe flamed the border lakes to create and maintain habitat for their "livestock," buffalo, caribou, moose, deer, and elk. They altered the Arrowhead, especially at local and regional levels, as much as pre-industrial Europeans had altered the Old World, and their primary tool was fire.[8]

William Denevan, a geographer at the University of Wisconsin, calls the long-held fallacy that the Europeans "discovered" in the Americas a natural, trackless, pristine wilderness that supported only a small population of benign natives living in harmony with a climax ecosystem "the pristine myth." George Perkins Marsh's seminal *Man and Nature,* possibly the first entry in the American lexicon of conservation and forestry, codifies this myth. In defense of his original title, "Man the Disturber of Nature's Harmonies," Marsh wrote to his publisher, Charles Scribner: "nothing is further from my belief, that man is 'part of nature' or that his action is controlled by the laws of nature; in fact a leading spirit of the book is to enforce the opposite opinion." Marsh's idea prevailed for more than a century.[9]

Even visionary Aldo Leopold and other influential early environmentalists ensconced the pristine myth as public policy when, in the *Leopold Report,* they directed to those charged with managing the national parks the following:

> As a primary goal, we would recommend that the biotic associations within each park be maintained, or where necessary recreated, as nearly as possible in the condition that prevailed when the area was first visited by the white man. A national park should represent a vignette of primitive America.
>
> The implications of this seemingly simple aspiration are stupendous. Many of our national parks—in fact most of them—went through periods of indiscriminate logging, burning, livestock grazing, hunting and predator control. Then they entered the park system and shifted abruptly to a regime of equally unnatural protection from lightning fires, from insect outbreaks, absence of natural controls of ungulates, and in some areas elimination of normal fluctuations in water levels. Exotic vertebrates, insects, plants, and plant diseases have inadvertently been introduced. And of course lastly there is the factor of human use—of roads and trampling and campgrounds and pack stock. The resultant biotic associations in many of our parks are artifacts, pure and simple. They represent a complex ecologic history but they do not necessarily represent primitive America.[10]

The pristine myth was central to the philosophy that inspired the 1964 Wilderness Act. Minnesota governor and ex-secretary of agriculture Orville Freeman described the wilderness movement as the recognition of value in "a primitive sanctuary undisturbed by the works of man," and while the Wilderness Act did protect certain areas from the ravages of industry, the pristine myth affected management decisions even as ecologists pointed out increasing problems.[11]

Many in the environmental movement also adhered to the pristine myth when industry tried to leverage tastier timber contracts by claiming that logging mimicked fire regimes and that increased logging, not prescribed burns, was the solution to fuel load problems. However, the fuel that needs to be removed is unmarketable for the most part, and the trees of greatest interest to industry, like white pine, tend to survive fires. Some environmentalists are afraid to crack the door to human activity in the wilderness, fearing those who would exploit resources will kick it all the way in. Others resist more aggressive wilderness management because they fear another Los Alamos fiasco or undesired results from clumsy bureaucratic hands.

The cultures and practices of today and those of Aboriginal Americans create vastly divergent landscapes. Aboriginals did not own land individually but managed it collectively, viewing land and herds as common resources, not as property or currency that could be possessed by an individual. Nor did they domesticate large animals like cows, sheep, or goats. Horses arrived with European settlers; natives did not use draft animals and so did not plow the soil, instead employing fire to clear land and digging sticks to plant seeds. Aboriginal farmers used "extensive" agricultural techniques, farming an area for a few years and then moving on to another site or creating habitat for favored species and then harvesting game in these places. They worked at a landscape level rather than in plots measured in acres or even hectares. Their use and alteration of the land left telltale signs much different from those Europeans would recognize.

Europeans—with private ownership of both land and animals, with draft animals, with metal implements, and with the wheel—used "intensive" farming techniques. Owners of animals and land fenced off pastures and corrals and built barns and silos to store feed and protect livestock from predators and weather. They plowed and manured rather than letting fields go fallow. They built levies and dikes and drained wetlands. All of these practices altered the landscape in predictable ways, ways that Europeans came to associate with farming. European farms looked like farms to Europeans, but aboriginal farms did not because their practices did not leave behind the same artifacts. European pioneers, coming into areas recently depopulated by epidemic diseases, often mistook aboriginal pasture for wild prairie or barrens and aboriginal "flocks" for wild herds. These rich, diverse landscapes are what most people think of when they talk about "pre-settlement" conditions.[12]

In the introduction to Stewart's long-delayed book—its ideas so revolutionary that although he completed it in 1950 he could not find a publisher until 2002—Henry T. Lewis and M. Kat Anderson describe the impact of aboriginal burning on this continent:

> While the fires of hearth and home have most often been of interest to anthropologists . . . the use of fire as a land management tool was universal and of critical importance in how humans related to environments. Setting fires to influence vegetation patterns was one of the most portentous achievements of our species; it literally shifted our status from foragers to cultivators of nature. . . . Indigenous burning practices were so successful in altering pathways of vegetation change that most of North America does not fit the definition of a pristine, uninhabited wilderness at the point of European contact. From the New Jersey pine barrens to the drier Douglas fir forests of the Pacific Northwest to the vast prairies of Canada and the United States, many vegetation types were profoundly affected by Native American burning.[13]

In the able hands of the aboriginals, fire created diverse and abundant landscapes, "optimizing" the land by initiating opportunities for multiple species and age classes and rich, varied regeneration. In northern Minnesota, tribal peoples created prairies for favored prey like antelope, elk, moose, and, at the forest's western edge, buffalo. They used fire in warfare, burned underbrush from dense forests to facilitate travel and hunting, torched brush to control insects, flamed swamps to eradicate disease, burned woodlands to lower fuel loads and prevent

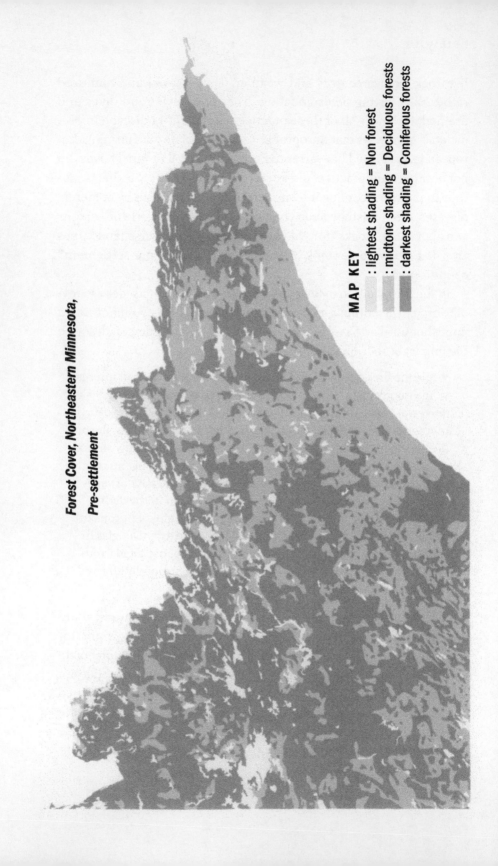

*Forest Cover, Northeastern Minnesota,*
*Pre-settlement*

**MAP KEY**

▨ : lightest shading = Non forest

▨ : midtone shading = Deciduous forests

▨ : darkest shading = Coniferous forests

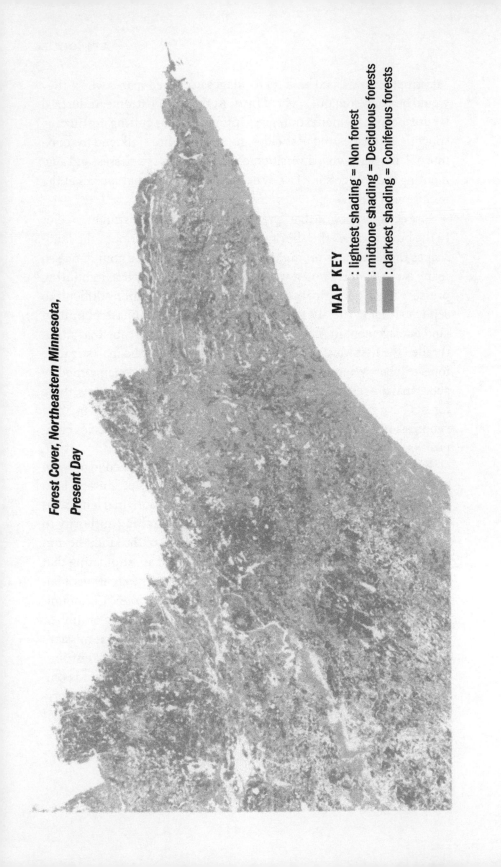

*Forest Cover, Northeastern Minnesota,*
*Present Day*

**MAP KEY**
: lightest shading = Non forest
: midtone shading = Deciduous forests
: darkest shading = Coniferous forests

catastrophic blazes, and built their villages in cleared spaces where they would be safer from unexpected fires. At the other extreme, industrial landscape management strategies—plowing, clear cutting, fertilizing, spraying herbicides and pesticides, suppressing fire—all tend to "maximize" land, narrowing diversity, creating uniform age classes, and augmenting the production of a few desired plant or animal species at the exclusion of others.

Fire ecologists argue that "pre-settlement" conditions ought to refer to the burn regimes the aboriginals had established, not to the landscapes those regimes produced. After all, much of the abundance so many early pioneers noted was due to the sudden decline in hunting pressure when aboriginal populations crashed, conditions difficult to replicate today. The aboriginal system was the first phase of human land management in America, and it created the landscape that so enthralled the first wave of pioneers. To a large extent, the majestic pine forests Robert Whiteside "discovered" were created and maintained by aboriginal fire regimes. In the absence of aboriginal fire, however, these forests have faltered, as reported in the 2003 Draft Forest Plan, "fire suppression and fire exclusion . . . dramatically changed species composition and structure of the forests."[14]

By the 1900s the destructive practices of industrialized logging in northern Minnesota forced a paradigm shift. The USFS promised a land management model that more closely resembled aboriginal land ownership styles. The United States formed an overarching authority to manage publicly owned wildlands—the resources of the land, the animals, the water, and the woods—for the benefit of all, stipulating that their use be sustainable over time. A few years after the creation of Superior National Forest, USFS manager George Cecil wrote: "Communities will depend on the National Forests for a steady supply of timber, and if we cannot meet this demand, we shall have failed in our mission. . . . [It is] doubly important that we regulate National Forest cuttings with the greatest consideration for the future welfare of the local communities." Cecil's letter clearly phrases the goals of the early forest service, its paradigm "sustained yield," its objective a continued harvest of natural resources at the maximum rate possible, its focus on the sustainability of the yield, not necessarily on the sustenance of the resource. It proposed an end to the cut-and-run days of the past in favor of maintaining communities and prolonging commerce.[15]

This goal remains elusive. Communities are being lost and families broken as children leave defunct lumbering towns in search of economic opportunity in urban centers. The absence of seed source and the effects of blister rust and, most importantly, deer browse ensure that big pine logging will not return to northern Minnesota. While the 2003 Forest Plan redefines the forest based on landscape ecosystems, with large areas designated "Mesic [Moist] White Pine–Red Pine Ecosystem" or "Dry White Pine–Red Pine Ecosystem," the draft plan acknowledges, "In 2001 clear cutting was still the dominant type of harvest occurring on the National Forests in Minnesota. . . . In order to improve the economy of northern Minnesota, the State attracted more mills. . . . Pulp mill capacity has increased since 1986."[16]

From 1986 to 1994 the volume of both old-growth (120 years or more) and pole-sized (less than 30 years) pine tumbled in Minnesota, a trend contrary to that of other Great Lake states and the East Coast. Today Minnesota contains less than one-tenth of one percent of the white pine it had before settlement. Economic rather than ecological realities have had a profound impact on Minnesota's national forest-lands.[17]

The Wilderness Act of 1964 created a new, more profitable economy based on recreation in many communities adjacent to wilderness and popular national forests, in part fulfilling the promise of stability dictated in the forest service charter. In 1986 recreation in the national forests generated $1.9 billion while timber brought in only $1.1 billion. Since the regulation of old-growth harvest in the Pacific Northwest the local economies have improved. Studies show that communities with strong environmental-protection programs also have the best job opportunities and the best climate for long-term economic development. In the Ely/Winton area property values and population have been growing steadily for more than a decade, with land values in some areas climbing at better than 20 percent each year.[18]

These positive reports cannot continue indefinitely, however. Wilderness aesthetics and recreation do not fulfill ecological considerations; they will not sustain the ecosystem. The havoc wreaked by the

July 4 storm, its destruction made worse by years of fire suppression, is the most obvious example. But the fact that white, red, and jack pine populations will continue to decline is another. The 1964 Wilderness Act, while important in protecting the forests from destruction by industry, does not guarantee the long-term viability of the wilderness ecosystems or the revenues they provide.

The 2003 Forest Plan, with its emphasis on ecosystem management, represents a departure from the sustained-yield or multiple-use paradigms that drove the 1986 Forest Plan. One premise of ecosystem management is that climate, physiography, soil, water, plants, animals, and humans interact to form ecosystems. Jack Ward Thomas, the chief forester when this theory came into play, wrote:

> My conception was that, compared with traditional approaches, ecosystem management involved more inclusive thinking at a larger scale, over a longer time frame, and considering more variables with the full recognition that people and the satisfaction of the needs and desires of people were a part of that approach. Inherent in the approach was the recognition that humans must exploit their environment in order to live. The question, then, was not whether to exploit the forest, but how to do so while saving what Aldo Leopold called all "the cogs and wheels."[19]

Ecosystem management is the USFS's first, halting step away from the pristine myth, the first practical admission that humans are part of the natural environment. However, this acknowledgement is made within the framework of modern humans only and fails to recognize the historic role humans have played in ecosystems. Ecosystem management does not mean that the USFS will be setting prescribed burns for ecological benefits in the BWCAW, nor does it mean there will necessarily be less resource extraction from the national forest. Because this paradigm recognizes that the land must serve human needs, industrial use of the national forests might well increase. Ecosystem management does acknowledge that understanding and protecting ecosystem processes is essential if there is to be a lasting supply of the materials and experiences that people require. Sustaining both ecological and economic systems is imperative, since they are inextricably linked and the well being of each is dependent on the well being of the other over time. But as conditions on the ground are altered by fuel build-ups or catastrophic events, as the reality of historic aboriginal management is more widely accepted, as more people trained in disturbance ecology make their way up the ladder within managing bureaucracies, policies will gradually shift to more of a restoration focus.[20]

The Wilderness Act's authors could never have imagined bombing the BWCAW with napalm, yet forty years later just that happened. Perhaps most amazing is the fact that there were no protests, no dissenters, no opposition to the plan, unlike just a few years earlier, when the question of using a single truck to haul boats over the Fourmile Portage had sparked rallies with hundreds of protesters on each side. The Magnetic Lake burn is the first quiet high-water mark of change, change that is just beginning and that will no doubt accelerate. A return to pre-settlement conditions may not be possible, and future management goals may focus more at the genetic level than at the landscape level.

With carefully developed policy that finds room for fire, for new growth, and for sustained yield, the nation's and the world's forests can satisfy the needs of many people—from tourists to loggers to environmentalists. A healthy forest through ecosystem management offers innumerable benefits to all.

Northern Minnesota is ecologically unique in that three bioregions intersect here, creating an overlap of edges. The hardwood pine forest of the Great Lakes—white and red pine with maple and oak hardwoods growing underneath—blends with the boreal/pine forest of the north— its arctic-studded spruces, balsam firs, and aspen birch stands—both of these encroached upon from the west by the Great Plains' semi-arid savannas. This layering allows researchers to see movement of the regional edges more quickly than they would from a few hundred miles inside a bioregion. Following the blow down, ecologists expected boreal forest to grow up under the tangled trees. Instead they are seeing oak and elm, hardwoods from a bioregion hundreds of miles to the south, signaling the advent of yet another catastrophe in the northland, one that is evolving more slowly than the sudden winds of July 4, 1999, but one that will ultimately be far more destructive. This catastrophe, global warming, promises to increase urgency for the adoption of restoration forestry practices.[21]

Computer models show a six- to ten-degree increase in average temperatures in just fifty years, about the same total warming that has occurred since the last ice age. Some climatologists predict that by the end of this century northern Minnesota will look much like Nebraska. Temperature increases have already changed the flora and fauna of the border lakes. The rate of change will only quicken.[22]

The resultant upheaval will demand ever more flexible management strategies. One direction is that, instead of trying to meet harvest levels of deer, or timber, or fish, land managers will be striving to restore native biodiversity to relative abundance reflective of pre-European conditions. Malcolm Hunter Jr. defines biodiversity as "the diversity of life in all its forms and at all its levels of organization." As a species survival strategy, biodiversity operates at four levels to improve the chance of species perpetuation: among species, among populations, among individuals within a population, and within individuals. The first two levels recognize the importance of genes, first genes that distinguish one specialized species from another and then genes that create an array of differences within a population. In operation, biodiversity allows different populations of the same species to occupy a wider range of environments than a single population could. At the third level, the differences between individuals allow for natural selection to benefit and strengthen a species.[23]

The future challenge will be to manage risk, not ecosystems as such, to optimize as the aboriginals did, to manage for options rather than for outputs. In response to this prediction, chief forester Jack Ward Thomas remarked wryly, "Of course, anything so new and radical as the retention of biodiversity as an overriding forest management objective to be achieved through 'ecosystem management' could be expected to set off a wave of consternation."[24]

Count among those resisting change corporations dependent on recreation or resources; bureaucracies like the USFS, which evolve with monumental slowness; and environmentalists and other members of the public who tend to cling to old ideas. Historically, environmental catastrophe has a way of precipitating change, but the ravages of climate change will come upon us very slowly, all of a sudden. Human lives are so short when compared with those of a tree or an ecosystem: as individuals we can't register environmental change. We risk becoming like the frog in a pan on the stove, who sits in the water as the flame slowly intensifies, until finally the water boils. We must rely on our history, on what we can learn about our present relative to our past, so that we can hope to feel the water slowly getting warmer and jump out of the pan in time. Led by science, using ecosystem management, restoration forestry—rather than rigid preservation, sustained yield, or multiple use—is the paradigm that will help mitigate the impending monumental environmental changes we will have to weather in the next millennium.

# Notes

**Notes to Introduction**

1. MacCleery, *American Forests*, 3.

2. Williams, *Americans*, 10.

3. Holmes, *Minnesota in Three Centuries*, 4:413–15; MacCleery, *American Forests*, 11; Williams, *Americans*, 3, 34.

4. Reynolds, *Lumber Production*, 1, 7.

5. Williams, *Americans*, 193.

**Notes to Chapter 1**

1. Daniel and Sullivan, *North Woods*, 60.

2. Bonnicksen, *America's Ancient Forests*, 43; Jacobson and Dieffenbacher-Krall, "White Pine," 39; Heinselman, "Fire in the Virgin Forests," 329–82.

3. Heinselman, *Boundary Waters Ecosystem*, 89.

4. Woodbridge and Pardee, *History of Duluth*, 564; Heinselman, "Fire in the Virgin Forests," 343.

5. Kozlowski and Ahlgren, *Fire and Ecosystems*, 200; Heinselman, "Fire in the Virgin Forests," 343; Sorden, *Lumberjack Lingo*, 30.

6. Heinselman, "Fire in the Virgin Forests," 343.

7. Kozlowski and Ahlgren, *Fire and Ecosystems*, 197; Heinselman, "Fire in the Virgin Forests," 347.

8. Heinselman, "Fire in the Virgin Forests," 358.

9. Cole, "Restoring Natural Conditions," 415.

10. Steen, *Origins of the National Forests*, 4.

11. Minnesota Legislature, Pine Lands Investigating Committee, *Report*, 55.

12. *Ely Times*, January 9, 1891; Minnesota State Forestry Board, *Sixth Annual Report*, 44.

13. Larson, *White Pine*, 298.

14. Olson, *Land Utilization*, 118; Minnesota Legislature, Pine Lands Investigating Committee, *Report*, 55.

**Notes to Chapter 2**

1. *New York Times*, "Unique Home for Rich Man," January 17, 1903.

2. *Ely Times*, March 6, 1891.

3. Thorton, *History of Pioneer Mine*, 18.

4. Ibid., 19.

5. Burnquist, *Minnesota and Its People*, 4:407.

6. *Vermilion Iron Journal*, January 22, 1891.

**Notes to Chapter 3**

1. *Vermilion Iron Journal*, July 14, 1892.

2. *Mississippi Valley Lumberman* 18 (November 21, 1890): 16; Larson, *White Pine*, 365.

3. Trygg, *Pioneer Lumbering*, 1.

4. Ibid., 4; *Ely Miner*, October 5 and November 5, 1898; "Proposed Mill, October

1889," blueprints, Whiteside materials, St. Louis County Historical Society, Duluth, MN.

5.  *Ely Miner*, February 8 and 22, 1899.

6.  *Ely Miner*, October 12, 1898, and May 5 and October 13, 1899.

7.  Ibid., June 21, 1899, and October 5, 1898; Trygg, *Pioneer Lumbering*, 1.

8.  *Ely Miner*, November 27, 1899; Trygg, *Pioneer Lumbering*, 2. The origin of the Three Spot is rather obscure. The first locomotive on the Duluth and Iron Range line was also known as the Three Spot, and both engines were built by the same company. While it does not appear that these two locomotives are one, the story of the first locomotive to come to the north country is worth a little digression.

The Duluth and Iron Range's Three Spot was originally built for a railroad in Brazil which then refused her. She was taken up the line to Duluth and put on a raft to be hauled over Lake Superior to Agate Bay, now known as Two Harbors:

"The lake was calm when the Ella G. Stone, the company tug named after George Stone's wife, started out with the scow carrying its precious locomotive cargo. Upon reaching Knife River, about twenty miles up the lake, a moderate northeaster began to blow. It soon increased to such gale proportions as to endanger the lives of the men. Tug Captain C. O. Flynn gave orders to the crew to stand by and be ready at his command to use an axe to cut the lines securing the tug to the scow, but fortunately this did not become necessary. In the words of William McGonagle, who was one of the men aboard, 'A kind providence and the excellent seamanship of Captain Flynn saved us the necessity of sending the Three Spot to Davey Jones' locker, and instead we sailed into the peaceful waters of Agate Bay and delivered our cargo safely on the rails that projected from the timbers at the shore line.'" King, *Missabe Road*, 24.

9.  *Ely Miner*, April 26, 1899; King, *Logging Railroads*, 108; Trygg, *Pioneer Lumbering*, 5.

10.  *Ely Miner*, October 5, 1898.

11.  Swallow and Hopkins's timber cruiser, Sven Olson, recommended that Good build a dam at Pipestone Falls, raise Newton Lake to the level of Fall Lake, hoist logs from Basswood into Newton, and then tow the booms directly to the mill. Good decided against this because it "involved a very long and difficult log towing operation . . . as well as the problem of hoisting at the Pipestone dam, all of which would have slowed up our logging operations." Good, "Fall-Basswood Lake," 2.

12.  Lake County Records, *O/Cont/308*, Two Harbors, MN; Forest Service Site No. 05–213, USFS Collections, Iron Range Research Center, Chisholm, MN; *Ely Miner*, March 31, 1900.

13.  Good, "Fall-Basswood Lake," 2.

14.  Ibid., 3; Trygg, *Pioneer Lumbering*, 10; *Ely Miner*, July 27, 1900.

15.  Trygg, *Pioneer Lumbering*, 3, 4. Linklater was a leader of his people, and his wife, *Thee-kee-wis*, or "woman of supernatural powers," was a prominent figure among the Ojibwe. Among whites she was known as Helen Linklater and was equally well respected. After the logging boom ended, John Linklater became one of the most effective game wardens in Superior National Forest's history.

16.  February 20, 1880, U.S. Survey General of Minnesota, Land Survey Field Notes, Minnesota Historical Society, St. Paul, MN (hereafter MHS). U.S. surveyor William A. Kindrid reported an American Fur Company Trading Post there; E. Matt Laitala, interview by Jeff Forester, October 15, 1991, tape and transcript, Wilderness Research Foundation, Ely, MN (hereafter WRF).

17.  MacCleery, *American Forests*, 17.

18.  *Ely Miner*, July 19, 1901; *Report of the Auditor*, 1900–1902, n.p.

19.  *Ely Miner*, April 20 and October 4, 1900.

20. Ibid., May 10, 1899, January 25 and March 22, 1901, February 28 and November 21, 1902, October 9, 1903, and August 17, 1914.

21. Ibid., October 6, 1899, and December 12, 1913; Ely Commercial Club, "Ely, Minnesota," 3. Howe faced challenges beyond those of constructing the Stony Tote Road. Stony River country was generally too rugged for the typical ice-road hauling done in other areas, making Howe almost completely dependent on the river to move his logs to the mill. Because the current slows through Birch, White Iron, Farm, and Garden Lakes, he most likely used horse headworks to tow his booms across the still waters that first year.

The next year the Torinus brothers brought in a much larger tug for Fall Lake, the *Cupid,* and put their old tug *Paul* to work on White Iron. *Cupid* was sixty feet long, had a twelve-foot beam, and drew seven feet of water. *Ely Miner,* January 5, April 20, and May 8, 1900.

22. *Ely Miner,* February 28, June 20, and August 1, 1902.

23. See the *Ely Miner,* May 17, 1899, for a full description of the steam crawler's first test winter; Williams, *Americans,* 209; Jacob Pete, interview conducted by John Esse, May 27, 1976, tape and transcript, MHS; Laitala, interview.

24. Leonard Costley, interview by Bruce Harding, August 3, 1957, Forest History Society, comp., Interviews with Pioneer Lumbermen, transcript, p. 10, MHS; *Ely Miner,* March 16, 1906.

25. *Ely Miner,* April 13, 1906.

26. Lake County Register of Deeds, *Reference o/m/183,* Two Harbors, MN. St. Croix filed for a $1 million bond issue on September 4, 1907, through the Minnesota Loan and Trust Company. See also Walt Okstad to F. B. Hubachek, December 16, 1986, in "Thematic Study," WRF files.

27. See *Ely Miner,* "Fires Bad," June 24,

1910, and "Forest Fires, Commissioner of the Forest Makes Statement," June 17, 1910, for details about the many fires and "Forest Fires, Doing Unestimable Damage in the Northwest," May 13, 1910, for effects on St. Croix specifically.

28. Pyne, *Year of Fires,* 71; Edward Hines Jr., interview by Jeff Forester, September 15, 1992, tape and transcript, WRF.

29. *Minutes of Annual Stockholders Meeting,* book 1, p. 202, Virginia and Rainy Lake Company records, MHS. Copy in WRF files.

30. Edward Hines to Thomas S. Whitten, November 21, 1910, Virginia and Rainy Lake Company records, MHS; Roaring Stoney Days Celebration, "Souvenir Booklet," 57; *Ely Miner,* "Mills Working," May 19, 1911.

31. Hill, *Frederick Weyerhaeuser,* 21.

32. Ibid., 4, 21.

33. Ibid., 14.

34. Henry Schoolcraft, who accompanied Lewis Cass on an exploration of the Northwest Territory in 1820, wrote the first description of Beef Slough: "We encamped on a long spit of naked sand, which marked its entrance to the Mississippi." Schoolcraft, *Personal Memoirs,* 389.

35. Williams, *Americans,* 205.

36. Blair, *Raft Pilot's Log,* 53.

37. Larson, *White Pine,* 135, 143. Larson describes the slough's operations in great detail; see also Williams, *Americans,* 206; Blair, *Raft Pilot's Log,* 53, 289.

38. Hidy, Hill, and Nevins, *Timber and Men,* 50; Williams, *Americans,* 206; Larson, *White Pine,* 140.

39. Steen, *Origins of the National Forests,* 4; Steen, *U.S. Forest Service,* 6.

40. Hidy, Hill, and Nevins, *Timber and Men,* 62.

41. *Ely Miner,* July 22, 1904.

42. Nute, *Rainy River Country,* 96; *Ely Miner,* March 30, 1906.

43. *Ely Miner,* May 16, 1902.

44. Corrigan, *Caulked Boots,* xi.

45. Christopher Thole, manuscript, 2, Northern Lumber Company records, MHS.

46. Frieas, *Empire in Pine*, 137; Williams, *Americans*, 218. For maps, see U.S. Bureau of Corporations, "Land Holdings," 188–216.

47. *Ely Miner*, "Buys Railroad: Edward Hines Concern Buys Swallow & Hopkins Railroad," May 5, 1911; King, *Logging Railroads*, 109.

48. *Ely Miner*, July 30, 1915; Thole manuscript, 3; *Ely Miner*, May 5, 1911; Lake Forest Enterprise, *Reference 366/ Deeds/404*, Two Harbors, MN.

49. Minnesota State Auditor, *Stumpage Reports*; Minutes of Meetings, Stockholders, 26, box 3, St. Croix materials, Virginia and Rainy Lake Company records, MHS; White, *Historical Sketches*, 13; Trygg, *Pioneer Lumbering*, 1; *Ely Miner*, May 5, 1911; King, *Logging Railroads*, 111.

50. *Ely Miner*, July 17, September 11 and 25, October 23, and November 27, 1914.

### Notes to Chapter 4

1. Peters, Hunn, Motivans, and Okstad, *Cultural Resource Management*, 213.

2. Laitala, interview.

3. Ibid.; Peters, Hunn, Motivans, and Okstad, *Cultural Resource Management*, 214.

4. Ryan, *Early Loggers*, 2:21.

5. Ryan, "Unwritten Laws," 34.

6. Sorden, *Lumberjack Lingo*, 65.

7. Ryan, *Early Loggers*, 2:55.

8. Roaring Stoney Days Celebration, "Souvenir Booklet," 27.

9. Jack Valentine to J. Wesley White, January 7, 1978, USFS Collections, Iron Range Research Center, Chisholm, MN.

10. Laitala, interview.

11. Ryan, *Early Loggers*, 2:30.

12. Ibid.

13. Wells, *Daylight in the Swamp*, 25; Ryan, *Lumberjack Queens*, 2.

14. Ryan, *Lumberjack Queens*, 3.

15. *Ely Times*, "Hell on Earth," February 24, 1893; *Ely Miner*, "White Slave," February 25, 1910; Laitala interview.

### Notes to Chapter 5

1. Zinn, *People's History*, 315.

2. Ibid., 331; Mitchell, "Union in the North Woods," 262.

3. Mitchell, "Union in the North Woods," 265.

4. Cahn, *Pictorial History*, 201; J. C. "Buzz" Ryan, interview by Jeff Forester, November 22, 1991, tape and transcript, WRF.

5. Kornbluh, *Rebel Voices*, 1; Industrial Workers of the World, *Proceedings*, 1.

6. Letterhead, labor files, WRF.

7. In Ely, one man, Abe Bloomenson, cashed the lumberjacks' checks for full value. Abe sold lumberjack clothes— woolens, fifty-pound canvas duck, caulked boots, pacs, and rubbers—and Abe was willing to keep a jack's money in a strong box while he was out caterwaul'n, thereby saving many a man from getting rolled in the streets, too full of drink to protect his hard-earned cash. After World War I Abe sold the store to one of his clerks, Billy Mills, who continued to act as lumberjack banker. The store has changed owners and locations but still operates in Ely and still sells the lumberjack brands of Filson and Carhart. Billy Mills Jr., interview by Jeff Forester, October 29, 1991, tape and transcript, WRF.

8. Enberg, "Lumbering and Labor," n.p.

9. Workers Socialist Publishing Company papers, 1910–14, box 1, p. 446, MHS; *Ely Miner*, June 13, 1913, and August 6, 1915.

10. Laitala, interview.

11. Lind, *Hearings*, 81.

12. Ibid., 104.

13. Ibid., 13, 73.

14. U.S. Congress, *Congressional Record*, 3821; Kornbluh, *Rebel Voices*, 255; Bird, Georgakas, and Shaffer, *Solidarity Forever*, 115.

15. Bird, Georgakas, and Shaffer, *Solidarity Forever*, 104.

16. Ibid., 149; Zinn, *People's History*, 345.

17. Mitchell, "Union in the North Woods," 268.

18. Ibid., 266.

19. Ibid., 272.

20. Ibid., 274.

21. Pete, interview.

22. E-mail to author, December 9, 2003.

**Notes to Chapter 6**

1. Axelrod and Phillips, *Every American,* 126.

2. Turner, *Significance of the Frontier,* 1; Axelrod and Phillips, *Every American,* 217.

3. Steen, *Origins of the National Forests,* 4.

4. Handy, *Official Directory,* 1107.

5. Carhart, *Timber,* 43. The first time the federal government tried to reserve trees from the logger was in 1800, when Congress authorized President John Adams to set aside timberlands to supply mast trees for the navy. Other forest reserve legislation came in 1818, 1820, and 1827, all to no avail, for the legislation protected the land in law only. On the ground locals ignored the laws, crossed reserve boundaries, and cleared the forests.

6. Dana, *Forest and Range Policy,* 76.

7. Lapham, "Forest Trees," 4:196–97; Lapham, Knapp, and Crocker, *Disastrous Effects,* 26; Perlin, *Forest Journey,* 354, 355; Williams, *Americans,* 372. Lapham's great-grandson, Ray Fenner, currently heads one of the Midwest's most active environmental protection groups, Superior Wilderness Action Network, or SWAN.

8. Pinchot, *Breaking New Ground,* 81.

9. Clepper, *Professional Forestry,* 16, 20, 135; Sparhawk, "History of Forestry," 705.

10. Clepper, *Professional Forestry,* 18; Hough, *Report Upon Forestry,* 7.

11. Dunnell, *Congressional Record,* 1772.

12. Miller, "Wooden Politics," 287.

13. Fernow, *Economics of Forestry,* 2–5.

14. Schurz, *Speeches, Correspondence, Political Papers,* 5:22–33, "The Need of a Rational Forest Policy, Address Delivered Before the American Forestry Association and the Pennsylvania Forestry Association, at Horticultural Hall, Philadelphia, Oct. 15, 1889."

15. Clepper, *Professional Forestry,* 103; Bowers, "Present Condition," 157.

16. Larson, *White Pine,* 300; *Ely Times,* "Special Agent's Report," February 6, 1891.

17. Larson, *White Pine,* 283, 294.

18. Clepper, *Professional Forestry,* 23; Arnold, "Congressman William Holman," 301–13.

19. Wilkinson, *Memorials,* 74.

20. Minnesota Legislature, Pine Lands Investigating Committee, *Report,* 56.

21. Andrews, *Recollections,* 294.

22. Hidy, Hill, and Nevins, *Timber and Men,* 137.

23. Pinchot, *Breaking New Ground,* 111.

24. Clepper, *Professional Forestry,* 27, 28.

25. Pinchot, *Breaking New Ground,* 118.

26. Ibid., 150.

27. Ibid., 83; Steen, *U.S. Forest Service,* 96; *Ely Miner,* December 18, 1903.

28. Williams, *Americans,* 220.

29. Hines, interview; Cronon, *Nature's Metropolis,* 184.

30. Minnesota State Forestry Board, *Third Annual Report,* 25.

31. *Ely Miner,* May 15, 1908.

32. Pinchot, *Breaking New Ground,* 255; Clepper, *Professional Forestry,* 40–42.

33. Pinchot, *Breaking New Ground,* 261.

**Notes to Chapter 7**

1. Stewart, *Forgotten Fires,* 130.

2. Andrews, *Recollections,* 275.

3. Minnesota State Forestry Board, *Second Annual Report,* 77.

4. Minnesota State Forestry Board, *First Annual Report,* 83.

5. Pyne, *Year of Fires,* 19.

6. Minnesota State Forestry Board, *First Annual Report,* 83.

7. *Ely Miner,* May 7, 1909.

8. Ibid., July 1, 1910.

9. Heinselman, "Fire in the Virgin For-

ests," 339; *Ely Miner*, "Forest Fires," May 13, 1910. At the first annual meeting of the Minnesota Fire Prevention Congress, held the following year, speakers presented the following facts: "Taking the experience of 1910 as a basis, if the structures destroyed were placed close together they would reach from Chicago to New York [and] every one thousand feet there would be an injured or maimed person, while every three-quarters of a mile would be a victim whose life had been sacrificed to the red plague." *Ely Miner*, November 17, 1911.

10. Cox, *First Annual Report*, 12; *Ely Miner*, September 27, 1912.

11. *Ely Miner*, May 26, 1911.

12. Ibid.

13. White, *Historical Sketches*, 1:n.p.

14. *Ely Miner*, January 9, 1914, and January 8 and May 14 and 21, 1915.

15. White, *Historical Sketches*, 2:n.p.; "Timber Survey—South Kawishiwi Project, 1917–18," USFS Collections, Iron Range Research Center, Chisholm, MN; Okstad, "Logging Industry Thematic Study," n.p.

16. F. P. Leggett to Forest Supervisor, "A History of Forest Conservation," November 21, 1925, Superior National Forest records, Duluth, MN.

17. White, *Historical Sketches*, 1:n.p., 4.1; *Ely Miner*, "Forest Notes," August 16, 1922; Holbrook, *Burning an Empire*, 33.

18. Minnesota Conservation Federation, *Factual Information*, 137; Leggett, "A History of Forest Conservation," Superior National Forest records; Peters, Hunn, Motivans, and Okstad, *Cultural Resource Management*, n.p.

19. Minnesota Conservation Federation, *Factual Information*, 140; Carhart, *Timber*, 138.

20. Carhart, *Timber*, 143, 146.

21. Leopold, "Wilderness and Its Place," 19. For a discussion of these events see Nash, *Wilderness and the American Mind*, 187. *Ely Miner*, May 2, 1921.

22. White, *Historical Sketches*, 12: n.p.

23. Ibid., 6:5.

24. Minnesota State Forestry Board, *Thirteenth Annual Report*, 25; Bachmann, *History of Forestry*, 7.

25. Clepper, *Professional Forestry*, 258. One by one the lumbermen who had logged the border lakes moved to the West Coast. In 1901, E. S. Howe left Tower to search the states of Oregon, Washington, and Idaho for timber. Robert Whiteside bought 26,000 acres of mahogany, rosewood, and cedar in Banderos Bay, Mexico, in addition to 13,000 acres of sequoia, the famous Calaveras Groves near Yosemite, some of the largest and oldest trees on the planet.

**Notes to Chapter 8**

1. Minnesota Conservation Federation, *Factual Information*, 119; Mitchell, "Union in the North Woods," 264; *Ely Miner*, February 8, 1907.

2. *Ely Miner*, March 15, 1912; *Final Decree, May 29, 1918*, St. Louis County Probate Court, Lake County Recorder's Office, Book Reference *E/misc./495*, Two Harbors, MN; Trygg, *Pioneer Lumbering*, 4; *Quit Claim Deed, March 11, 1921*, Lake County Recorder's Office, Reference *21/D/191*, Two Harbors, MN.

3. *Minutes of Meetings*, Virginia and Rainy Lake Company records, box 3, book 1, p. 243, MHS.

4. Frank Swan, "Whiteside Office Calendar," WRF files.

5. Clepper, *Professional Forestry*, 256.

6. Olson, *Land Utilization*, v, 59, 163, 241.

7. Proescholdt, Rapson, and Heinselman, *Troubled Waters*, 5; Minnesota Conservation Federation, *Factual Information*, 1.

8. Baldwin, *Quiet Revolution*, 203.

9. Proescholdt, Rapson, and Heinselman, *Troubled Waters*, 11; Carhart, *Timber*, 30.

10. Heinselman, *Boundary Waters Ecosystem*, 114.

11. Ibid., 115.

12. Ibid., 125.

13. *Ely Miner*, July 21, 1916.

14. Ibid., December 30, 1921; Carhart, *Na-*

*tional Forests*, 126; Dave Tucci, USFS, to Jeff Forester, June 28, 1994, WRF files.

15. Searle, *Saving Quetico-Superior*, 70.

16. White, *Historical Sketches*, 16:n.p.

17. *The Wilderness Act*, Sec. 4, Public Law 88–577, 88th Cong. (September 3, 1964).

18. Heinselman, *Boundary Waters Ecosystem*, 120.

**Notes to Chapter 9**

1. Ahlgren, *Lob Trees*, 137.

2. Ibid., 107; Lee Frelich, interview by Jeff Forester, September 25, 2001, transcript, WRF.

3. Ahlgren, *Lob Trees*, 108.

4. Ibid., 108, 110.

5. Carhart, *Timber*, 183.

6. Gary Brown, interview by Jeff Forester, September 7, 2001, transcript, WRF.

7. Heinselman, "Fire in the Virgin Forests," 375; *Wilderness Act*, Sec. 2(c) (1).

8. Paul Tiné, interview by Jeff Forester, March 7, 2003, transcript, WRF; USDA Forest Service, "Boundary Waters Fuel Treatment," 1, 3.9–18.

9. Tiné, interview.

10. Murkowski, *Hearings*, 3.

11. USDA Forest Service, Region 9, "National Visitor Use," 6, 9; Tiné, interview.

12. Pyne, *America's Fires*, 38.

13. USDA Forest Service, "Boundary Waters Fuel Treatment," 4.

14. Ibid., 1.

15. Ibid., 5.

16. Ibid., 7.

17. Frelich, interview.

**Notes to Epilogue**

1. Berry, *Home Economics*, 11.

2. USDA Forest Service, "Draft Environmental Impact," p. 1–9, 1–11.

3. Crosby, *Ecological Imperialism*, 196; Wilson, *Earth Shall Weep*, 18.

4. Smith and Meredith, *Coming of the Pilgrims*, 52; Bradford and others, *Homes in the Wilderness*, 16; Mann, "1491," 42.

5. Dobyns, *Native American Historical Demography*, 1; Thornton, *American Indian Holocaust*, 45; Krech, *Ecological Indian*, 93; Stannard, *American Holocaust*, x.

6. Krech, *Ecological Indian*, 84.

7. Stewart, *Forgotten Fires*, 112.

8. Krech, *Ecological Indian*, 98.

9. Mann, "1491," 42; Marsh, *Man and Nature*, xxiii.

10. Leopold, Cain, Cottam, Gabrielson, and Kimball, *Wildlife Management*, 32.

11. Baldwin, *Quiet Revolution*, vii.

12. Wilson, *Earth Shall Weep*, 23.

13. Stewart, *Forgotten Fires*, 3.

14. USDA Forest Service, "Draft Environmental Impact," p. 3.5–5.

15. Quoted in Clary, *Timber and the Forest Service*, 27; George H. Cecil to the Forester, May 6, 1911, USFS, Dist. 1, S & ST District, Policy 1911–1913, R1, 63-A 209/82498, National Archives and Records Services, Washington, DC.

16. Ralphe Bonde, interview by Jeff Forester, December 15, 1994, transcript, WRF; USDA Forest Service, "Draft Environmental Impact," p. 3.4–7, 3.4–9.

17. Jan Green to Joe Barnier, District Ranger, Gunflint Ranger District, September 5, 1994, WRF files.

18. Rice, *National Forests*, 56; New York Times News Service, "Oregon Timber Town Enjoying Renaissance," reprinted in the *Chicago Tribune*, October 18, 1994; *Minneapolis Star Tribune*, October 12, 1994.

19. Hunter, *Maintaining Biodiversity*, x.

20. Cleland, Crow, and Probst, "Multiple Objectives," 108.

21. Frelich, interview.

22. Bonnicksen, *America's Ancient Forests*, 41.

23. Hunter, *Maintaining Biodiversity*, 3.

24. Ibid., x.

# Bibliography

Ahlgren, Clifford and Isabel. *Lob Trees in the Wilderness*. Minneapolis, MN: University of Minnesota Press, 1984.

Andrews, Christopher C. *Recollections of Christopher C. Andrews, 1829–1922*. Cleveland, OH: Arthur H. Clark Company, 1928.

Arnold, Ron. "Congressman William Holman of Indiana: Unknown Founder of the National Forests." In Steen, *Origins of the National Forests*, 301–13.

Axelrod, Alan, and Charles Phillips. *What Every American Should Know About American History: 200 Events That Shaped the Nation*. Holbrook, MA: Adams Media Corporation, 1992.

Bachmann, Elizabeth M. *A History of Forestry in Minnesota: With Particular Reference to Forestry Legislation*. St. Paul, MN: Minnesota Division of Forestry, 1965.

Baldwin, Donald N. *The Quiet Revolution: Grass Roots of Today's Wilderness Preservation Movement*. Boulder, CO: Pruett Publishing Co., 1972.

Berry, Wendell. *Home Economics*. New York: North Point Press, 1987.

Bird, Stewart, Dan Georgakas, and Deborah Shaffer, eds. *Solidarity Forever: An Oral History of the* IWW. Chicago: Lake View Press, 1985.

Blair, Walter Acheson. *A Raft Pilot's Log: A History of the Great Rafting Industry on the Upper Mississippi, 1840–1915*. Cleveland, OH: The Arthur A. Clark Company, 1930.

Bonnicksen, Thomas M. *America's Ancient Forests: From the Ice Age to the Age of Discovery*. New York: John Wiley & Sons, Inc., 2000.

Bowers, Edward A. "The Present Condition of the Forests on the Public Lands." *Publications of the American Economic Association* 6 (January and March 1891): n.p.

Bradford, William, and others of the Mayflower Company. *Homes in the Wilderness*. Margaret Wise Brown, ed. Hamden, CT: Limnet Books, 1988.

Burnquist, Joseph A. A. *Minnesota and Its People*. 4 vols. Chicago: S. J. Clark Publishing Company, 1924.

Cahn, William. *A Pictorial History of American Labor*. New York: Crown Publishers, 1972.

Carhart, Arthur H. *The National Forests*. New York: Alfred A. Knopf, 1959.

———. *Timber in Your Life*. New York: Lippincott Company, 1955.

Clary, David A. *Timber and the Forest Service*. Lawrence, KS: University Press of Kansas, 1986.

Cleland, David T., Thomas R. Crow, and John R. Probst. "Multiple Objectives and Ecological Tools." In Stine, *White Pine Symposium*, 108ff.

Clepper, Henry. *Professional Forestry in the United States*. Baltimore, MD: Johns Hopkins University Press, 1971.

Cole, Glen F. "Restoring Natural Conditions in a Boreal Forest Park." *Transactions of the Forty-Ninth North American Wildlife and Natural Resources Conference*. Washington, DC: U.S. Fish and Wildlife Service, 1984.

Corrigan, George. *Caulked Boots and Cant Hooks*. Ashland, WI: Northword, Inc., 1976.

Cox, W. T. *First Annual Report of the State Forester*. St. Paul, MN: State Printer, 1911.

Cronon, William. *Nature's Metropolis: Chicago and the Great West*. New York: W. W. Norton and Co., 1991.

Crosby, Alfred W. *Ecological Imperialism: The Biological Expansion of Europe, 900–1000*. New York: Cambridge University Press, 1986.

Dana, Samuel T. *Forest and Range Policy*. New York: McGraw-Hill, 1956.

Daniel, Glenda, and Jerry Sullivan. *The North Woods of Michigan, Wisconsin, Minnesota and Southern Ontario*. San Francisco, CA: Sierra Club Books, 1981.

Dobyns, Henry F. *Native American Historical Demography: A Critical Bibliography*. Bloomington, IN: Indiana University Press, 1976.

Dunnell, Mark. *Congressional Record*. 47th Cong., 1st Session, March 9, 1882. Vol. 13.

Ely Commercial Club, United States Forest Service. "Ely, Minnesota: Gateway to the Superior National Forest." In *The Playground of a Nation*. Ely, MN: The Club, 1927.

Enberg, George. "Lumbering and Labor in the Lake States." *Minnesota History* 36.5 (1959): 153–66.

Fernow, Bernard. *Economics of Forestry*. New York: Thomas Y. Crowell & Co., 1902.

Frieas, Robert F. *Empire in Pine: The Story of Lumbering in Wisconsin, 1830–1900*. Madison, WI: State Historical Society of Wisconsin, 1951.

Good, Herb G. "Fall-Basswood Lake Logging Railroad." In Trygg, *Pioneer Lumbering*, 1–5.

Handy, Moses P., ed. *The Official Directory of the World's Columbian Exposition, May 1st to October 30th, 1893*. Chicago: W. B. Conkey Company, 1893.

Heinselman, Miron. *The Boundary Waters Wilderness Ecosystem*. Minneapolis, MN: University of Minnesota Press, 1996.

———. "Fire in the Virgin Forests of the Boundary Waters Canoe Area, Minnesota." *Quarterly Research* 3 (1973): 329–82.

Hidy, Ralph Willard, Frank Ernest Hill, and Allan Nevins. *Timber and Men: The Weyerhaeuser Story*. New York: Macmillan, 1963.

Hill, William Bancroft. *Frederick Weyerhaeuser: Pioneer Lumberman*. Minneapolis, MN: McGill Lithograph Company, 1940.

Holbrook, Stewart H. *Burning an Empire: The Story of American Forest Fires*. New York: Macmillan Company, 1945.

Holmes, Frank R. *Minnesota in Three Centuries, 1655–1908*. New York: The Publishing Society of Minnesota, 1908.

Hough, Franklin B. *Report Upon Forestry Prepared Under the Direction of the Commissioner of Agriculture, in Pursuance of an Act of Congress Approved August 15, 1876*. Washington, DC: Government Printing Office, 1878.

Hunter, Malcolm L. Jr., ed. *Maintaining Biodiversity in Forest Ecosystems*. New York: Cambridge University Press, 1999.

Industrial Workers of the World. *Proceedings of the First Convention of the I.W.W.* New York: New York Labor News Company, 1905.

Jacobson, G. L., and A. Dieffenbacher-Krall. "White Pine and Climate Change: Insights from the Past." *Journal of Forestry* 93:2 (1995): 39–42.

King, Frank A. *Minnesota Logging Railroads*. San Marino, CA: Golden West Books, 1981.

———. *The Missabe Road: The Duluth, Missabe and Iron Range Railroad*. San Marino, CA: Golden West Books, 1972.

Kornbluh, Joyce L., ed. *Rebel Voices: An IWW*

*Anthology.* Chicago: Charles H. Kerr Publishing Company, 1988.

Kozlowski, T. T., and C. E. Ahlgren, eds. *Fire and Ecosystems.* New York: Academic Press, 1974.

Krech, Shepard III. *The Ecological Indian.* New York: W. W. Norton & Company, 1999.

Lapham, Increase A. "The Forest Trees of Wisconsin." *Transactions of the Wisconsin State Agricultural Society* 4:196 (1855).

Lapham, Increase A., J. G. Knapp, and H. Crocker. *Report on the Disastrous Effects of the Destruction of Forest Trees Going on So Rapidly in the State of Wisconsin.* Madison, WI: Atwood and Rublee, 1867.

Larson, Agnes M. *White Pine Industry.* Minneapolis, MN: University of Minnesota Press, 1949.

Leopold, Aldo. "The Wilderness and Its Place in Forest Recreation Policy." *Journal of Forestry* 19:7 (1921): 718–21.

Leopold, Aldo, S. A. Cain, C. M. Cottam, I. N. Gabrielson, and T. L. Kimball. *Wildlife Management in the National Parks: The Leopold Report.* Washington, DC: National Park Service, 1963.

Lind, John. Papers. *Hearings: Labor Troubles 1917.* Vol. 1. Minnesota Historical Society, St. Paul, MN.

MacCleery, Douglas W. *American Forests: A History of Resiliency and Recovery.* Durham, NC: Forest History Society, 1992.

Mann, Charles C. "1491." *Atlantic Monthly* 289:41 (March 2002): 41–54.

Marsh, George Perkins. *Man and Nature.* Cambridge, MA: Belknap Press of Harvard University Press, 1965.

Miller, Char. "Wooden Politics: Bernard Fernow and the Quest for a National Forest Policy." In Steen, *Origins of the National Forests,* 287–300.

Minnesota Conservation Federation. *Factual Information Concerning Minnesota's National Forests.* Hopkins, MN: The Federation, 1943.

Minnesota Legislature, Pine Lands Investigating Committee. *Report.* St. Paul, MN: Pioneer Press Company, 1894.

Minnesota State Auditor. *Stumpage Reports, 1900–1920.* Minnesota Historical Society, St. Paul, MN.

Minnesota State Forestry Board. *Annual Reports, 1895–1926.* The Pioneer Press Company. St. Paul, MN.

Mitchell, Stacy. "Union in the North Woods: The Timber Strikes of 1937." *Minnesota History* 56:5 (Spring 1999): 262–77.

Murkowski, Frank H. Committee on Energy and Natural Resources, U.S. Senate. *Hearings Before the Subcommittee on Forests and Public Land Management.* 106th Cong., September 15, 22, and 23, 2000.

Nash, Roderick. *Wilderness and the American Mind.* 3rd Edition. New Haven, CT: Yale University Press, 1967.

Nute, Grace Lee. *Rainy River Country: A Brief History of the Region Bordering Minnesota and Ontario.* St. Paul, MN: Minnesota Historical Society Press, 1950.

Okstad, Walter A. "Logging Industry Thematic Study." Heritage Annual Report, USFS, Duluth, MN, 1982. Copy in USFS Collection, Iron Range Research Center, Chisholm, MN.

Olson, Floyd B. *Land Utilization in Minnesota: A State Program for the Cut-over Lands.* Minneapolis, MN: University of Minnesota Press, 1934.

Perlin, John. *A Forest Journey: The Role of Wood in the Development of Civilization.* Cambridge, MA: Harvard University Press, 1991.

Peters, Gordon R., John O. Hunn, Karen A. Motivans, and Walter A. Okstad. *Cultural Resource Management on the Superior National Forest.* Duluth, MN: USDA Forest Service, 1982.

Pinchot, Gifford. *Breaking New Ground.* Washington, DC: Island Press, 1947.

Proescholdt, Kevin, Rip Rapson, and Miron L. Heinselman. *Troubled Waters: The Fight* for the Boundary Waters Canoe Area Wilderness. St. Cloud, MN: North Star Press, 1995.

Pyne, Stephen J. *America's Fires: Management on Wildlands and Forests.* Durham, NC: Forest History Society, 1997.

———. *Year of the Fires: The Story of the Great Fires of 1910.* New York: Viking Press, 2001.

*Report of the Auditor of the State to the Legislature of Minnesota, for the Two Fiscal Years Ending July 13, 1900, and July 31, 1902.* St. Paul, MN: The Pioneer Printing Company, State Printers, 1903.

*Report of the Auditor of the State to the Legislature of Minnesota, for the Two Fiscal Years Ending July 31, 1908.* Minneapolis, MN: Syndicate Printing Co., 1908.

Reynolds, R. V. *Lumber Production 1869–1934.* Washington, DC: USDA Forest Service, 1936.

Rice, Richard E. *National Forests: Policies for the Future.* Washington DC: The Wilderness Society, 1989.

Roaring Stoney Days Celebration Historical Committee. "Souvenir Booklet." Ely, MN: Ely-Winton Historical Society, 1958.

Ryan, J. C. *Early Loggers in Minnesota.* 3 vols. Duluth, MN: Minnesota Timber Producer's Association, 1975, 1976, 1980.

———. *The Lumberjack Queens.* Duluth, MN: St. Louis Historical Society, 1983.

———. "The Unwritten Laws." In *The Timber Producer's Bulletin* (March 1990): 34–36.

Schoolcraft, Henry Rowe. *Personal Memoirs of a Residence of Thirty Years with the Indian Tribes on the American Frontiers.* New York: AMS Press, 1978.

Schurz, Carl. *Speeches, Correspondence, Political Papers.* New York: Knickerbocker Press, 1913.

Searle, Newell R. *Saving Quetico-Superior: A Land Set Apart.* St. Paul, MN: Minnesota Historical Society, 1977.

Smith, E. Brooks, and Robert Meredith. *The*

*Coming of the Pilgrims: Told from Governor Bradford's Firsthand Account.* Boston, MA: Little, Brown and Company, 1964.

Sorden, L. G. *Lumberjack Lingo.* Spring Green, WI: Wisconsin House, 1969.

Sparhawk, William Norwood. "The History of Forestry in America." In *Trees: The Yearbook of Agriculture.* Washington, DC: U.S. Department of Agriculture, 1949.

Stannard, David E. *American Holocaust: Columbus and the Conquest of the New World.* New York: Oxford University Press, 1992.

Steen, Harold K., ed. *The Origins of the National Forests: A Centennial Symposium.* Durham, NC: Forest History Society, 1992.

———. *The U.S. Forest Service: A History.* Seattle, WA: University of Washington Press, 1976.

Stewart, Omer C. *Forgotten Fires: Native Americans and the Transient Wilderness.* Norman, OK: University of Oklahoma Press, 2002.

Stine, R. A., ed. *White Pine Symposium Proceedings: History, Ecology, Policy and Management.* St. Paul, MN: Minnesota Extension Service, University of Minnesota, 1991.

Thornton, Russell. *American Indian Holocaust and Survival: A Population History Since 1492.* Norman, OK: University of Oklahoma Press, 1987.

Thorton, Charles H. *The History of Pioneer Mine, Arrowhead County of Minnesota.* Fond du Lac, WI: Berndt Printing Company, n.d.

Trygg, J. William. *Pioneer Lumbering, Winton, Minnesota, 1898–1922.* Ely, MN: The Author, 1966.

Turner, Frederick Jackson. *The Significance of the Frontier in American History.* New York: Henry Holt & Co., 1920.

U.S. Bureau of Corporations. "Land Holdings of Large Timber Owners." In *The Lumber Industry,* 188–216. New York: Arno Press, 1972.

U.S. Congress. *Congressional Record.* 65th

Cong., 2nd Session, 1918.

U.S. Department of Agriculture, Forest Service. "Boundary Waters Fuel Treatment, Final Environmental Impact Statement." Duluth, MN: USDA Forest Service, 2001.

———. "Draft Environmental Impact Statement, Forest Plan Revision, Superior National Forest." Duluth, MN: USDA Forest Service, 2003. Available: http://www.fs.fed.us/r9/chippewa/plan/revision/draft/plan_snf/index.shtml

U.S. Department of Agriculture, Forest Service, Region 9. "National Visitor Use Monitoring Results, August 2001, Superior National Forest." Milwaukee, WI: USDA Forest Service, 2001. Available: http://www.fs.fed.us/recreation/programs/nvum/reports/year1/R9_Superior_final_082001.doc

Wells, Robert W. *Daylight in the Swamp.* Ashland, WI: Northword, Inc., 1987.

White, J. Wesley. *Historical Sketches of the Quetico-Superior.* 16 vol. Duluth, MN: USDA Forest Service, 1967–1974.

Wilkinson, Rev. William. *Memorials of the Minnesota Fires in the Year 1894.* Minneapolis, MN: Norman E. Wilkinson, 1895.

Williams, Michael. *Americans and Their Forests: A Historical Geography.* New York: Cambridge University Press, 1989.

Wilson, James. *The Earth Shall Weep: A History of Native America.* New York: Atlantic Monthly Press, 1998.

Woodbridge, Dwight E., and John S. Pardee. *History of Duluth and St. Louis County.* Chicago: C. F. Cooper and Company, 1910.

Zinn, Howard. *A People's History of the United States.* New York: Harper Perennial, 1980.

# Index

## CREDITS

Unless otherwise noted, photographs are from Minnesota Historical Society collections.

frontispiece and pages 32 and 47: courtesy of the Iron Range Historical Society
pages 34, 36, 45, and 52: Lake County Historical Society
pages 54–55: map by Matt Kania, Map Hero, Inc.
page 110: Library of Congress
page 170: copyright 2004 Star Tribune / Minneapolis–St. Paul
pages 175, 189: courtesy Superior National Forest, USDA Forest Service
pages 184–85: maps by Tim Loesch, Minnesota Department of Natural Resources

*The Forest for the Trees* was designed and set in type at the Minnesota Historical Society Press by Will Powers. The text type is Whitman, designed by Kent Lew. *The Forest for the Trees* was printed by Sheridan Books, Ann Arbor, Michigan.

Printed in the USA
CPSIA information can be obtained
at www.ICGtesting.com
JSHW082201140824
68134JS00014B/365

9 780873 516501